TIME to STOP PRETENDING

TIME to STOP PRETENDING

by

STEPHANIE RODRIGUEZ

Paul S. Eriksson, *Publisher*
Middlebury   **Vermont**

10 9 8 7 6 5 4 3 2 1

Library of Congress Cataloging-in-Publication Data

Rodriguez, Stephanie.
   Time to stop pretending / Stephanie Rodriguez.
       p.   cm.
     ISBN 0-8397-8060-5
     1. Rodriguez, Stephanie.   2. Abused women — United
States — Biography.   3. Homeless women — United
States — Biography.
   I. Title.
HQ809.3.U5R65   1993
362.82′92′092--dc20
   [B]   93-8299
                                                             CIP

To
the memory of
my father
Donald W. Rigby

CONTENTS

Introduction

IT IS SAID that for battered women the road to freedom from abuse is paved with the shock of realization, self-determination and empowerment. Stephanie Rodriguez's story of her journey out of the abyss of degradation, suffering and abject terror is unique and courageous. And in her telling, the reader comes to understand the agony of the thousands of women and children who struggle against tremendous odds to flee abuse and find safety.

Stephanie's life story is singularly horrific and heartbreaking, encompassing as it does suicide, bloody beatings, child abuse, rape, nearly unutterable humiliation, selfishness and unbelievable cruelties. Right now, hundreds of thousands of women and children are living through experiences similar to Stephanie's. The prevalence and severity of domestic abuse and its effects on the victims are staggering, and the costs to society monumental. For instance:

- Every fifteen seconds, an act of domestic violence occurs.
- 50% of all willful homicides of females are committed by a past or present intimate partner.
- 20% of all murders (more than 4000 each year) in the U.S. are domestic-violence related.
- 63% of all boys, aged 11 to 20, who are arrested for murder, have killed the man who was assaulting their mother.
- Up to 50% of all homeless women and children in the U.S. are fleeing domestic violence.
- After being sheltered, 31% of abused women in New York City returned to their abusers primarily because they could not locate longer-term housing.
- 15–25% of all females who are battered are pregnant.
- The March of Dimes reports that more babies are now born with birth defects as a result of the

mother being battered during pregnancy than from the combination of all the diseases and illnesses for which we immunize pregnant women.

- Battering is the single major cause of injury to women—more frequent than auto accidents, muggings, and rapes combined.
- 85% of batterers watched domestic violence occur in their own homes as children, and/or experienced physical/sexual abuse themselves.
- Every five years, there are more women killed in domestic-violence incidents in the U.S. than there were U.S. casualties in Vietnam.

What is so inspiring about *Time to Stop Pretending* is that this battered woman, Stephanie Rodriguez, and her children, escaped with their lives and through this mother's strength created a new existence of peace and normalcy.

I agree with Stephanie that "soft words spoken at the kitchen table can't counteract the hopelessness and terror" any more than the soft words spoken at the diningroom table in our local battered women's shelter. I know that the quiet references to therapy and counseling, the plans for

"case management" and referrals, the legal advo-
cacy and restraining orders, hot meals and clean,
warm beds have not had the effect of immediate
resolution and empowerment.

Yet, I have seen masks slip off and hearts hope
and women cry tears to unfreeze a soul, when
simply sharing my own story of abuse, escape and
a new life. And I say to you, Stephanie Rodriguez,
with this book, this brave act of baring your soul
and shame, of breaking the silence, you will touch
many abused women, and in so doing will pass on
to them the incandescent light of empowerment.

Mikki Patterson, Co-Chair
Battered Women's Task Force
of the National Coalition
Against Domestic Violence

TIME to STOP PRETENDING

Preface

IT HASN'T BEEN easy to write this book. So much of my past embarrasses me. But I have swallowed the embarrassment long enough to tell everybody the things I never wanted to tell anybody.

My original intention was to help other battered women see a way out of their situations. I imagined my own story, told in my own words, might hold an answer for them. The memories I've endured in order to accomplish this telling, however, all but convinced me of the futility of such an aspiration. Battered women are a difficult, if not impossible, group to rescue. That mustn't stop us from trying, I suppose. It doesn't stop me from wishing.

I wish I could reach every woman who has been beaten by her husband or boyfriend today. I wish I could sit at her kitchen table with her and tell her that I know.

Of course that's silly. Soft words spoken at her kitchen table can't counteract the terror and hopelessness eating at her heart. Any more than this book can. I knew this before I started, but I was compelled to try and write some part of the big truth that might help some woman, somewhere, to get out of an abusive situation.

I remember all the people who tried so hard, again and again, to help me out. It's hard to explain why it never worked, but a story told to me by a friend who used to be a train engineer helps a little: One night, on a long stretch of track, he noticed a figure far ahead. On the tracks, he thought. For a long time the distance between the train and the figure appeared to remain the same. He wondered if it wasn't some sort of optical illusion. After a while, however, the train began to gain on the figure, and soon my friend was close enough to see the terrified and exhausted dog, running for all he was worth, looking back over first one shoulder, then the other, at the tremendous monster bearing down on him. He blew the whistle. The dog increased his speed, but was unable to maintain the pace. Finally the train ran him over.

My friend expressed amazement that the dog hadn't simply jumped to the side, out of harm's way. There was, after all, only a small rail on either side of him; nothing at all to keep him on those tracks.

I hate that story. I think I know why the poor dog wasn't able to save himself. He was so involved in the business of staying ahead of the monster on his tail that he couldn't possibly conceive of another thing. He didn't have time to reason out that a single step in either direction would save him.

It's a lot like that for the battered woman who can see only the monster on her tail. All the people on the sides of the track — the friends, family, and social workers, calling out instructions, trying their damnedest to talk her out of there, are only so much more clamor. They stir up dust, and add to the confusion.

I've run the frantic run for my life. I've tuned out the well-intentioned clamorers on the side. I realize the unlikelihood that what I say will, of itself, prompt a woman to get out of what she's already in. But I would hope to encourage her and strengthen her resolve. True escape must come — if it comes — from within her.

I wrote this book, then, for the daughters — the ones not yet caught up in it, the future battered women. This is the story that their own mothers might tell them. It's the story I want my own daughters to remember.

I come from a long line of battered women, and like each of them, I grew into my mother's warped sense of identity, confusing vulnerability with femininity. I also mistook crazed and brutal beatings for impassioned, jealous love. I found a man who was every bit as impassioned and jealous as my own father, and settled down to bask in the love. It was all I needed. That and a good health-care plan.

I'm one of the lucky ones. I did not follow my mother's footsteps all the way. But whatever it is that has to happen inside a woman to change her mind, happened inside me, and I got out.

I didn't just walk out; it doesn't go like that. It has to be the right time. Unfortunately, my right time didn't come until after I'd had eight kids, and then, it found me with no money, no food, and no place to go. The time was right, nonetheless, and I went.

There was a different kind of worry for awhile, a less personal danger, but as far as I could tell, life on the streets and in the shelters of New York wasn't any better or worse than life with him had been. Finally, with the aid of the Salvation Army, we escaped.

At first I worried every day that he would find us, but years passed and he didn't. More years passed and I grew cocky. "Let him find us," I thought nonchalantly. "What can he do to us now?" I was beginning to forget.

Memory came back in a flash when my oldest daughter came home with a bright red welt on her cheek.

"It was just one slap, Mom," she answered when I questioned her. "He didn't beat me up or anything."

Panic gripped me. We hadn't gotten out soon enough. The danger had followed. My daughter was going to do this anyway. Just as I and my mother and her mother had done it. What about my other daughters, I wondered. Will they too?

"He really loves me, Mom," she explained. "He just can't control his. . . "

I stopped listening then. I already knew the words.

She had forgotten. Completely forgotten how her father and I had 'loved' each other. Forgotten what I'd told her about the 'love' that my own parents had shared. Maybe I should tell her again. Maybe there were a lot of things that I should tell her.

It was then that I began to think about what I knew, about what I might say to women who found themselves in a situation similar to mine. There wasn't much that would help.

I examined my life, from every possible angle, looking for the secret, the way out. What, I wondered, had made me leave him, that day, after all those years? Needless to say, I never figured it out. For me, a certain something had clicked inside me and everything was different. To this day, I don't know why. It had just happened.

Getting into the whole ugly mess in the first place hadn't just happened, though. That's what this book is about — how I got into it, and what it was like.

I've told the story in small pieces, each of which stresses a particular point important to an understanding of the abuse. In the process, I have found, I think, a larger truth. I find that my husband didn't do what he did to me by himself. He had plenty of help. His parents, my parents, our society all worked together. They set us up, from the start, to become the abuser and the abused.

This is a story painful to recall and embarrassing to recount. It is a story that aspires to save our daughters. It may, at least, help others to understand them. It is a story that needs telling.

There are a few people without whom the telling would not have been possible. There's Gary Templeton, without whose encouragement I never would have started, and without whose financial and moral support I never could have finished; Anne Williams, who went far beyond the duties of a teacher to help me understand how to do what I wanted to do; and the Erikssons, Peggy and Paul, who, recognizing my inexperience, exercised great patience in guiding me through the publishing process. My heartfelt thanks to all of them.

I've changed some of the names in my story for obvious reasons, but the story remains real. I've kept it that way.

For the daughters.

1

Better Off Godless

I USED TO live differently from the way I do now. I used to wish I was dead. I really wished it. The kind of wishing that you never speak out loud.

I had a god back then, and so alternatives to life, but I never prayed to that god for death. I was afraid he'd take offense at such prayers and punish me. Perhaps even with a longer life. He was an ironic sort of god.

I didn't pray or speak aloud of my death wish. I staggered through one miserable day after another, collecting abuses, storing them away—admission fee to some later paradise.

I had been in the process of suicide since I was twelve years old, smoking too much, frequenting the wrong place at the wrong time, and playing with fire, knives, and occasionally guns. By far the deadliest weapon with which I toyed was the one that I married. It nearly got me.

My husband beat me up — often. Sometimes quite badly. In all honesty I can't remember caring much at the time, but I do now. Now it's important to me that, if nothing else, people don't hit me.

Back then, it was just part of God's plan for me. I didn't know why God wanted me beat up, but considering his Joan of Arc plan, I guess I thought myself pretty lucky.

My husband was a Catholic. He didn't go to church or pray or wear a button or anything. He just said he was a Catholic and we had lots of kids.

I was an unfit mother back then. Ideas like social duty or parental responsibility were foreign to me. I gave no thought to what my kids ate or said or did, and they ate and said and did the worst. It never occurred to me to monitor what they learned on TV or from their peers or from their father. I figured God had planned these kids, he could take care of them. I was just passing through on my way to paradise.

I remember when that began to change. It was during a nasty ordeal that God had planned for Valerie, my ten-year-old daughter. She had lost her notebook. Her father was helping her find it with his belt. This in itself was not unusual, but this time, while he was beating her, she turned around and fell. The belt struck her face. He got mad and hit her harder. Said she was trying to make him look bad. When he finished, he explained that this process would be repeated every five minutes until the notebook was found, and closed the door. We all searched under and behind everything. Five minutes passed — no notebook. It began again. He wasn't careful where he hit her this time. I tried once to get his attention. He swung the belt at me, striping my arm and neck.

The second round over, he was gone again. We were frantic. Where was the stupid notebook?! I pictured him eagerly timing this interlude, waiting just outside the door, biting his finger to keep from snickering, hoping we wouldn't find the notebook. Maybe he'd hidden it himself.

Time sped. Valerie began pleading with me in breathy, wet little whispers to please help her. In desperation, I started praying to God to please help her. "God please help Valerie. . . . Please God help Valerie."

Right on time, he burst through the door and grabbed her wrist. God wasn't going to help Valerie. For the first time in my life, I went against the silly "plan." I ran.

Beside the refrigerator was a two-and-a-half-foot piece of two-by-two — a club he kept in case of prowlers. I grabbed it and ran back to Valerie. Her legs no longer held her. She was on her knees. He was a maniac, cussing and whipping wildly. God wasn't doing a thing to stop it.

A quick "whack" from the two-by-two stopped it, right then. Just like that, it ended. No praying or waiting for a disinterested god to take action. I did it myself with one quick whack.

Unfortunately, I couldn't muster another. I dropped the board; he picked it up. The rest of the night was pretty messy. It involved emergency people. But a change had begun.

I grew away from my god. The further I got from him, the closer I got to myself and my family, to reality. The less I depended on him, the more I depended on me. I even decided that paradise could wait, at least until I got my kids grown.

They needed me. I was quicker to action on their behalf than was God. I didn't know why. Maybe it was all the same to him, but I was in no hurry to see any of my kids off to paradise, no matter how nice a place it was.

I took it upon myself to take the kids away from that life. We didn't immediately spring into a better one, however. There were months of homelessness, hunger, sleeping in subways, the blessed humiliations of shelter life. We did and saw things that I'm sure none of us care to remember, or will ever forget — things that convinced me, ultimately, that if there is a god, he's deaf, dumb, and blind, or worse, he doesn't care.

We're here now, many miles away. We've been here for six years. Six years since we've lived that life or seen that man. We're growing strong, getting better.

I want to live now. After all, I've nowhere else to go. I wish I could live forever.

I'm careful now. I monitor, for myself, what my kids do and say, and eat, what they learn from TV and peers, and from their mother. I don't wait for God to do anything anymore, and nobody ever hits us.

That's the way I wrote it the first time, my whole life story, happy ending included, in a thousand words or less. In those thousand words I uncovered the single villain responsible for all my woes. Not only did I find the culprit, I eliminated it and we lived happily ever after.

The only trouble is that those thousand words tried to cover twenty-eight years of my life, an impossible task. The story wasn't right. It was entirely true; it just wasn't the entire story.

This little thousand-word life story was not a flop, however. On the contrary, it remains my favorite piece of writing, for it did a wonderful thing. It caused me to take a good hard look at what really happened during those twenty-eight years. It gave me, not the answers, but the questions to my life. Why had I been in the process of suicide most of my life? Why did I stay so long with someone apparently hell-bent on killing me? How did I get with him in the first place? Just what was wrong with me?

I worked my way through the thousand-word story little by little, looking more thoroughly at each statement made or implied. I uncovered brand new villains at every step and abandoned them along the way. I found new people and things to blame for the problems in my life. By the time I was finished, I believe that I did find the true culprit — and there was only one — responsible for all my woes. Perhaps in the process I wrote an interesting story.

2

Learning to Pretend

THE P.T.A. LADIES mobbed us as soon as we walked into the annual "Welcome back to school" supper. My mom was a higher-up in their organization and they'd been waiting for her. Seems Francis Klinger had seen her in the supermarket two days ago and the news had spread fast. Now they wanted all the details. They had to know about the tape stretched across her nose and about the bruises on her face.

Mrs. Vintner took the pan of baked beans from my mother's hands and put it in mine. She sent her daughter Barbara with me to arrange it on the table with the other dishes. "And take the foil off the top," she called after us. Barbara was the same age as I. We were starting the fourth grade.

"Wow, man!" she whispered, excited. "What happened to your mom's face?" I shrugged and walked faster. I left Barbara talking at the table and hurried back toward the women.

I stood next to my mother as she described her imaginary dive into the shallow end of a swimming pool. It was so detailed, so real. I wondered, as I peered into her bruised and bloodshot eyes, if she didn't believe it herself. Heck, I almost believed it, and I knew better. I'd been there when my father grabbed the back of her hair. I'd seen him bash her face, again and again, into the door jamb. And after he'd gone, I'd caught the blood in my lap as I cradled her sobbing head and waited for Grandma to come and get us.

Although I much preferred her story, something inside me ached, ever so slightly, as I watched her laugh at her pretend foolishness.

The women finally tired of the story, offered routine sympathies, and drifted one by one back to the buffet table at the far end of the gymnasium.

I stared up at her. She held her head high. Her eyes wandered the room. Everywhere but at me. She squeezed my hand hard and swallowed deep breaths.

I knew my father's promises by heart already, and wasn't really surprised when things kept on pretty much as usual between them. She continued to explain away any physical evidence.

Then, just after Easter, during a minor incident that was more words than anything else, something unusual happened. He was yelling at her across the kitchen table as we ate. It wasn't unusual that her fear grew with the volume of his voice, or that her terrified eyes kept pace with his fury. It certainly wasn't surprising that we all flinched when his hand flashed across the table and struck her. What was different this time, was that, for her, it ended there. The fear disappeared. Her eyes stopped darting and stared blankly at nothing. She didn't raise an arm to shield her face from the second or third blows; She didn't seem aware of them.

After he left, she didn't cry or need anything. She closed herself in her room and didn't answer when I knocked or when I called softly through the door. She finally came downstairs, wearing old shorts and sandals, with her hair tied back, as if she were going to clean house. She grabbed each of us — my sisters, my brother and me, and kissed our faces. She hugged us too hard, for too long a time, whispering softly about "the time to stop pretending," and then she left.

My father came home toward evening and climbed the stairs to recite his standard apology. He looked strange when he came down. Not at all angry, maybe even scared. There was a sheet of yellow paper in his hand. It shook as he spoke.

"What time did your mother leave, Debbie?" he asked my oldest sister.

She still wasn't home when we went to bed. He waited up.

I had no idea what time it was when Debbie woke me. "Shhhh," she cautioned. I followed her to the stairs and we crouched behind the banister. There were policemen in the living room. One of them had his hand on my father's shoulder in a sorry kind of way. My father was shaking. His face was in his hands and I couldn't make out what he was saying. Something about God and a lot of dirty words.

"What is it, Debbie?"

"Shhhh!" She didn't look at me.

Suddenly he was mad. "Get out!" he screamed at the policemen. "Just get the hell out!"

One of them placed a card on the table and they left.

The door closed and my father began searching for something. On the mantel, in the fruit bowl on the table, under the couch cushions. "Lying bastards!" he muttered. "Dirty lying bastards!" Finally, he gave up, snatched the card from the table, and was out the door, hair uncombed and muttering still.

I followed Debbie down the stairs and stood beside her in the door. The look on her face scared me. The living room seemed bigger than usual. Cold, dim, and particularly empty. A chill blew in through the open door and a slight drizzle speckled the dark tile floor. Outside under the streetlight, a fine mist swirled, and a crumpled paper bag skipped aimlessly around the empty street.

The yellow paper that had shaken in my father's hand poked out from beneath the sofa. I picked it up.

"I'll be waiting for you in Hell, my love," it began.

I didn't understand most of the note. Debbie was no help. She read it silently, placed it on the couch between us, and went back to staring expressionlessly out the open front door. I drew my arms and legs up into my gown and snuggled into the corner of the sofa.

I don't know how long it was before I jumped awake to the sound of my father's voice. It wasn't night anymore, but it wasn't quite day either.

"Where's Mommie?" I asked.

His eyes and nose were swollen and red. His face was blotchy. "Go on upstairs now and go to bed." He spoke softly. "It's not time to get up yet." I heard a tremble in his voice. The remains of a small fire glowed in the ashtray.

"I smell smoke," I complained.

"It's all right," he said, gently. "Go to bed."

I sensed great importance.

Once in bed, I tried to stay awake, tried to realize the significance of my father crying downstairs, but the sobs melted into a hazy, dreamlike chant, and lulled me into a deep sleep, far, far away.

Nobody actually said she was dead on that first day, but there were signs. Friends and neighbors ran in and out of our house, bringing food and sorry looks. Grandma bought us new, black clothes, and my father didn't go to work.

He didn't go to work on the second day either, and there was even more company. My brother and I were out in the yard when my father called us inside. In the doorway, he whispered angrily, "For God's sake, have the decency to stop bouncing that damn ball while your poor mother lays dead!"

My brother froze, stared at him for a few seconds, and broke into a furious run through the house and up the stairs.

I didn't go into the kitchen; the P.T.A. ladies were in there. From the stairway I heard them discussing, once again, my mother's face.

"I guess her face is really a mess." whispered Mrs. Vintner. "They're having a hard time fixing her up for viewing."

"What a shame," one of them clucked. "So beautiful."

"Why don't they just have a closed casket?" Francis Klinger wondered.

"Well they might have to, but I'd hate to see it happen; she's got so much family."

Upstairs, Grandma had all of my mother's best outfits laid out on the bed, comparing them, deciding.

That night I dreamed of a movie I'd seen about a mother who returned home from a deserted island after years of supposedly being dead.

I didn't cry at the funeral.

At this point in my examination, it seemed easily apparent I had been in the process of suicide because it was the way my mother had chosen to go. Perhaps I had been so traumatized by her death that I had never really gotten over it. In reality, however, that seems unlikely. The worst thing about my mother's death was the realization it wasn't the worst thing. Not for me anyway. The sun came right on up the next morning and the next, and after five miserable days and a funeral I was back at school reciting the pledge of allegiance to the flag. All that remained of the previous week's horror was a lingering anxiety, a vague sense that a distant but very important fastener had somehow come unsnapped.

Within six months, my oldest sister had run off with a sailor, my father had drunk up all the insurance money, and my mother's best friend had taken her place as my father's wife. Her name was Joanne. She talked a lot about what we ought to remember and what we ought to forget. She wanted us to forget the bad things and remember only good times when we thought of our mother. It was more healthy she said. No sense rehashing all the problems of a life gone by. It made sense, I suppose, that she concentrated particularly on my father, as he seemed particularly haunted by bad memories. The mistake in Joanne's philosophy became evident when, less than a year into their marriage, he forgot some of the things he should have remembered and beat her up. We never saw her again.

My father's next wife was Ruthie. Ruthie placed a great deal of importance on marriage, and sticking to it, and God's plan, and things like that. I guess people today would say she had family values. I know she had something. Something very powerful. She was much more than a stepmother to me. I felt whatever it was that she gave off, and after a while, so did my father. It was those years with Ruthie that gave my father back his humanity, and ultimately gave me back my father.

3

Mama

I LIKED RUTHIE. She treated me special. Always asked me to help her do stuff. I did. I helped because I liked being around her. I suspected that she asked me for the same reason. We were folding laundry one afternoon when out of nowhere she asked me the strangest question.

"Did your Daddy ever hit you?" she asked, pulling a towel from the basket.

"No," I answered easily, thinking what a silly question it was.

She sat on one end of the couch and I sat on the floor at the other end. The two laundry baskets sat between us.

"That's good." She placed the folded towel on the towel pile in the center of the sofa.

"Did he ever hit your mom?" She looked at me carefully.

"I don't know," I answered, wishing she wouldn't ask things like that. "I can't remember too much."

"Hmm." She stopped folding for a minute and looked me in the eye. "What about Joanne?" she asked. "Did he ever hit her?" Joanne was my father's second wife, the one before Ruthie—the one who had left us the very first time my father hit her. Left and never came back.

I didn't answer right away and Ruthie looked at me suspiciously. "Did he hit her?"

"No," I lied, trying to sound like this, too, was a silly question. "Why would my dad hit somebody?" I asked innocently.

She picked up another towel and shook it out. "I was just asking, Honey."

Ruthie had been with us for about a year when she asked me to call her Mama. We were peeling potatoes at the kitchen table, when out of the blue, she asked me what I had called my mother.

"Mommie," I told her.

"Well, how 'bout you call me Mama," she said. Just like that.

I stopped peeling. I knew that I couldn't call Ruthie Mama. My sister Debbie would never let me do that. Debbie hated Ruthie. She'd even accused her right out loud once of taking over our mother's house. Ruthie had pointed out that we'd moved twice since she died, and in all likelihood our mother had never even seen this house. That didn't stop Debbie's resentment.

Ruthie was looking at me. "It's not like I'd be taking her place," she said. "You wouldn't call me Mommie. That would be her special name." This was impossible. I didn't want to hurt her feelings. I didn't want her to go away. To tell the truth, I would have liked to call her 'Mama.' But I didn't want to be a traitor, either. I looked down at my potato and said nothing.

"Well," she said finally, "Don't worry about it. You don't have to." I looked at her face. She put her hand on my shoulder. "But if you ever want to," she smiled. "I'd like it a lot."

From then on, if I wanted her attention, I tapped her shoulder or just started talking. I thought it would be rude to call her Ruthie after that. I couldn't call her anything else.

She was home with just my brother and me one Saturday night watching TV when, once again, everything went crazy. We all jumped when the back door rattled.

"It must be Daddy." I laughed. It was.

He didn't notice any of us as he staggered to the cabinet that held the record player. He put on a record and sat down on the floor with his back against the cabinet and his head on his bent knees.

Donny and I stood, instinctively, to go upstairs. But poor Ruthie, she didn't know any better. She walked over and turned down the music.

"The kids are watching a show," she explained when he looked up, incredulous.

Donny mumbled that it was all right, that we were tired anyway.

"Yeah." I nodded agreement. "Why don't we all go to bed?" I stretched for effect.

She said everything was all right, and that we should finish watching our movie. She really didn't know.

He fumbled with the stereo knobs while she spoke. When he found the volume knob, she reached, automatically, to turn it down again. He grabbed her hand. With his other hand, he turned the music off.

I didn't argue when he sent Donny and me out to "get something to eat." I didn't say that it was past midnight, and I didn't look at the half-eaten sandwiches and kool-aid we were leaving on the coffee table. I took the money my father held out and grabbed my brother's hand. A woman on TV screamed in terror at the wolfman as we left. The sound made the hair on my neck stand up. I didn't look at Ruthie. I couldn't.

Donny and I didn't speak as we swung our feet in the fountains on Woodruff Place. I don't know what he was thinking, but I thought about the day Ruthie had asked me if Daddy hit Joanne. Why did I lie to her? I lied to her for my father; I wished desperately that I hadn't. Maybe it would be different now if I hadn't lied that day.

When it seemed like it had been long enough, we went home.

The front door was locked. I hated to go around the side of the house in the dark; there were always snails. I didn't think about them now. I stumbled over the record player. It lay, pitifully crippled, in the yard just below the side window.

It was just inside the back porch that I saw the blood-smeared plastic glove, and panic built in my throat. I swallowed and pushed the kitchen door open. Behind me, my brother made little "oh" sounds all the way through the house. The kitchen looked all right, and the dining room. But at the entry to the living room we stopped short. The coffee table was slightly out of place. Grape Kool-Aid from an overturned glass puddled on top of it, threatening to drip over the edge. Ruthie's "just polished" hardwood floor had been spared that indignity only by the absorbency of our sandwich bread. The horror on channel four had long since ended, leaving only the station's test pattern to illuminate the tiny red sprinkles splattered across the T.V. screen. I knew what they were, even before I saw the blood-soaked towels next to the end table.

I ran through the kitchen after Donny, and caught him just before he made it out the door.

"We should wait here," I whispered. He just kept making those noises.

We stood together by the wall phone in the kitchen and after a while it rang.

We were in Grandma's kitchen before Donny broke down all the way. I wished he would be quiet. I couldn't think with him making all that noise. I wondered where my father was, and how Grandma had known to call us. I tried very hard not to wonder about Ruthie.

She was already through the worst of it, and going to be all right, before anybody told us she'd been shot. When she was officially out of danger, Grandma took us to see her in the hospital. On the bus ride over, we passed the county jail where my father was. I didn't look at it.

The needles attached to her arms didn't keep her from hugging us.

The tears began as soon as she touched me. I didn't want her to let go of me; I didn't want to let go of her. More than anything, I did not want Ruthie to go away, as I knew she would have to now.

"I'm sorry," I said a million times.

"It's not your fault," she answered.

When she was well, Ruthie dropped all charges against my father, claimed it was an accident, and came home to us.

Always, after that, I called her Mama.

After that, things changed. For the better, I suppose. Life certainly got better for my father and his new wife, and Ruthie only grew dearer to me. Things settled down and eventually calm became the norm around our house.

But calm was strange to me.

I found it impossible to get used to the new quiet that had taken over. It almost annoyed me, and I wonder if it wasn't just a matter of looking elsewhere for excitement that I left home so early.

Excitement, it turned out, was easy to find. Just before my sixteenth birthday, a guy named Lou moved into the house next door.

4

Getting Started

EVEN NOW I'M confused and a little embarrassed when I think of how I came to be with my husband.

For sure I fell in love when I was sixteen. The question is, was it with the mysterious and good-looking young man who had moved in next door to my parents, or was it with his car?

It was a '69 Dodge Dart convertible, white with a black top. He called her Candy, and kept her nice and shiny.

I had seen him before he got the car, and while he was undeniably handsome, he'd seemed, to me, dark-natured, mysterious and just plain scary. I'd always pretended not to feel him staring at me.

My friends said he liked me. They thought he was cute, his car was cool, and I should go for it.

Behind the wheel of that car he did become more cute than handsome; happier-seeming, and a little less scary. Still, my interests were based more on what my friends said I should be interested in than anything else. Whatever the reason, now when he looked at me, I looked back.

I'd never had a boyfriend before and wasn't sure how to go about it. I needn't have worried — he knew it all. He offered, one afternoon, to teach me to drive his car, and that was it. I was outclassed, overwhelmed and, in three months' time, what had begun as a dream ride in that car had become an ongoing nightmare in an apartment across town where I lived with this dark man who owned my life. He told me what to do and what to think. I did it and thought it. I didn't mind. That's the way adults did things. It *was* easier, and besides I couldn't think of anything else I really wanted to do at the time.

At first, when my friends visited, they joked that I was infatuated with the car. He didn't like that, and made sure everyone knew he didn't like it. After a while they stopped joking about the car, but he didn't like something else they did or said. Finally they stopped visiting us.

The first time he hit me it was for curling my hair. I was walking to the corner store to buy some things before he got home from work when he pulled up beside me. I got into the car and he accused me of planning to meet someone at the store. Why else would I have curled my hair, he demanded. I objected. He threatened to wait outside the store for whoever it was and kill him when he came out. I said he was ridiculous. He slapped me. I cried, but somewhere in me I thought it was all very romantic. I couldn't wait to talk to my best friend Sharon. I was dying to tell her. She would love this. It was so exciting. Me, who'd always been so immature, living just like a grownup.

It was a thrill that wore off quickly. By my seventeenth birthday, I was thoroughly disgusted with life and didn't care if I never took another breath. It never occurred to me that anything could or ever would be different. My life wasn't mine and I was damned tired of living it.

I never did learn to drive the car and it became, to me, just something else to wash.

When he came home from work one Monday evening and announced that he'd made appointments for blood tests and a marriage license for the next day, I didn't say anything. It worried me deeply, secretly, but I didn't say anything.

All week I kept thinking that something would surely happen to stop this if it wasn't supposed to be. Everything would work out in the end. If things went as he planned, all I could hope for was that the end would come soon.

None of that shows in the snapshots taken outside the church. No sign of bitter disillusionment. Nothing in my smile hints at the helplessness that was my new adulthood, or at the all-consuming disappointment with life.

One would never guess from the happy faces that the man had already broken my nose once, or that he had, in a fit of rage, hit me with his car.

Sometimes he hit me because he was high. Sometimes he hit me because he wasn't high. That's not what he said, though. He said he hit me because I showed "disrespect," a term I quickly

grew to hate for it meant something different every time he used it.

Whatever his reasons, he hit me more and more often, and less and less regretfully.

After we were married, people — first my sister, then my friends, then his friends — began to comment on the fact that I was rarely without some bruise, or cut, or broken bone. He said they were all gossips, and that we were moving to New York where people weren't always nosing into somebody's business. Three months after our wedding, we did just that.

It was a whole other world — loud, and fast, and scary as hell. Lou, who called himself a body/ fender man, but who had worked only sporadically, and then in factories and warehouses (body shops gave him asthma), became so busy on the streets every day that he could no longer find the time for a regular job. He stopped working altogether. We lived with his mother, Maria. She spoke no English. I spoke less Spanish. Spending all day every day alone together, however, we eventually came to speak the same language. It was neither English nor Spanish, but combined the two and added a series of hand and body *gestures. We got along well. I did everything she told me, she complained constantly about how American I was, and I liked the way it sounded.*

After a while, I came to relate to life in New York. It was a place that seemed more in tune with the way I'd always lived. I understood — sometimes.

5

Sounds of the Game

WE SAT ON the stoop at 156th street and Cauldwell. The police at the forty-second precinct in the South Bronx called this place the "hot block." To me it was home — the neighborhood.

The stoop was filled to capacity. The two "stoopers" blocking the entrance got up as needed to allow other people access to the door. Maria sat between her daughter, Marilyn, and me, with her hand on the back of a baby stroller, monotonously pushing it out and pulling it back over the concrete, long after its passenger, my nineteen-month-old daughter, had fallen asleep.

We all sat in the same stooping fashion with our knees bent sharply up. This left a little gap between my shorts and my leg through which sweat, from behind my knees, trickled down, causing me to shift uncomfortably. It may have been the pregnancy that made it seem hotter than usual, but judging by the amount of shifting going on around me, I doubted it.

Eight neighborhood guys played basketball ("shirts 'n skins") in the school yard kitty-corner to us. The sounds of the ball bouncing off the pavement, hitting the backboard or occasionally rattling the chain-link fence, and the shouts of "Foul!" or "Hey, Tito! Open! I'm open!" were familiar and comfortable.

Down the block, three groups of girls were jumping rope to three different sets of lyrics. "Fudge, fudge, call the judge" and "Cinderella dressed in yella" blended with the excited shouts of the boys exploring the abandoned building opposite us, to provide quite peaceful background music, to which my mother-in-law chattered incessantly. In her Spanish tongue, even my shortcomings sounded kind of pretty.

Somewhere between 4:00 and 4:30, Maria paused in her musical beratements to note Ray stumbling around the corner. Ray was one of those addicts who cleaned the bathrooms at the welfare office in exchange for his check. He was thirty-two, lived with his mother, and had been trying since forever to get off the junk. He was doing all right now; he'd come from a hundred-dollar-a-day habit down to one free fix every other day at the methadone clinic on 149th Street.

This must've been a free-fix day because he was really having it out with the "no parking" sign in front of our building.

We speculated for a while as we watched him, on whether or not junkies can sleep standing up; on what enables them to sway and bend so low, almost to the ground, without falling; and on just what it is about the junk that makes their legs itch so much. Ray cussed the sign, kicked it and tried to pull it out of the ground, but when a punch at it drew blood from his hand, Marilyn went to get his mother. We took turns trying to reason with him until she got there.

Blood dripped from his hand in a slight but steady stream, then splattered about the sidewalk as he waved his arms wildly, inviting his opponent to take the next shot. His opponent, though, no matter how he provoked, with threats, insults, and even slanders upon its mother, never once

responded with anything more than, "NO PARK-
ING THIS SIDE OF STREET Mon. Wed. Fri."
Ray, even under the powerful influence, must've
figured out that he had hurt himself with the one
punch. He wasn't throwing any others. It appeared to be a standoff.

His mother arrived in bathrobe, rollers, and
tears; tears of concern or shame, I couldn't say,
but there were plenty of them, mixed with a lot of
shouting.

At this point, it seems the sign whispered some
insult about Ray's mother. He attacked it with a
new vigor. "That's my mother," he lurched at it
"you son of a bitch!" His mother saw this as a cue,
and dropped promptly to her knees praying—
loudly. Marilyn and I avoided each other's eyes,
trying to prevent swallowed snickers from erupt-
ing into bursts of uncontrolled laughter.

The other women on the stoop eventually went
to the aid of the mother and son in crisis. I put my
foot on the stroller to keep it from rolling and
settled back to enjoy the show. Ray's mother remained knelt in prayer while the others struggled
comically to break his choke hold on the sign. Just
when I thought sure they had him, everyone

froze. Everyone—the guys, the kids, Ray, the women—was suddenly dead still. All the dribbling, playing, fighting, and praying ceased. Everything just stopped. The faces shared a single expression, as though, simultaneously, they'd remembered something that they wished they didn't know. My daughter bolted upright in the stroller, and the baby in my womb jumped.

A sound had done this—had grabbed everyone in this way. A quick "thud." It was not a loud noise but an extremely powerful one. A sound unlike any I'd heard before, yet strangely, instinctively, familiar—apparently to all of us, for there was silence, absolute silence, for a time. We were frozen in the moment; the instant went on and on.

Finally, a whispered "Ai Dios mio" broke the spell, triggering a confused stirring about in which jumpropes and basketballs were dropped, fights and contests were forgotten, and people, young and old, were reminded of something—something ancient and sacred; something ominous; something which, in that instant, could not be denied.

Almost in unison we headed in the direction of the thud. "Aww, shit, man!" Ray whined, turning back to throw up.

Tony, a seventeen-year-old neighbor boy, lay on the sidewalk. He didn't look broken or twisted the way you would expect after a six-story fall, but there was something odd about the tilt of his head. None of the gruesome gore associated with such a violent end; a fist-sized puddle of bright red blood was all that had spilled from him. His eyes were open, but obviously empty by the time we reached him.

It's not like we knew the kid; we didn't, (he wasn't much for hanging out) but every one of us felt his death — hard, close to our own.

It had something to do with a human bond, some residual of evolution. That sound his body made on impact had called to something basic in each one of us. It had communicated the fact that one of us was damaged irreparably. It was familiar in the sense that the bones that had shattered were like our bones; the lungs that had punctured and hissed were just like our flimsy lungs; the heart that had quivered and stopped was just exactly like our quivering, stoppable hearts. The link was undeniable. The sound of our mortality mocked us.

Death was among us—the same death that threatened each of us every day. Those of us who lingered, who stood around the body hoping, hoping . . . hoping right up until the paramedics pulled the sheet over his face, wanted that boy to make it. We wanted him to beat death, for all of us.

They took Tony away and we dispersed as the fire department cleaned the mess. I don't think any of us just went back to what we were doing. I followed my inlaws up the five flights to the apartment. I thought about all the things that can happen to any of us, my babies included. All I could offer my children were vulnerable little bodies, that could carelessly fall from a roof one day, or be thrown from a roof, or, worse yet, that could jump from a roof. It was scary as Hell.

There was much to guard against in this game, absolutely no chance of defeating the opponent. Still, we, the players, had no choice but to play, and found ourselves once again on the stoop.

It was eight-thirty now, and cooler. A bunch of neighborhood boys were shouting "Jones" at each other across the school yard. A group of girls were sitting on the stoop down the block. Occasionally one of them would shout something to get the boys' attention and they would all laugh. The sound of the old men slapping dominoes onto a card table under the street light, and their shouts of "Double six, the Devil! It's closed, ha ha, it's closed" blended with the giggles of the young couples exploring the abandoned building opposite us, to provide quite a peaceful background music. To which my mother-in-law chattered incessantly.

6

Thwack!

I LAY AWAKE in the darkness of the small apartment, and listened as playful rodents scurried across mangled linoleum.

I lay, as I had every night in the three weeks since the baby's birth, with my arm dangled over the side of the bassinette, my hand on her back. I worried that she might stop breathing for no reason. I'd heard stories about new babies who did that. More than that though, I worried that the rats that sometimes bumped the legs of the bassinette would one night climb up those legs, to Marie. I'd heard stories about that, too.

I'd already panicked once tonight. Snatching the baby up, I had leapt to my feet on the bed, and turned on the light, waking my husband. His reaction had suggested that the definite consequences of disturbing him again far outweighed any possible consequences of darkness. I turned the light off.

I lay there afraid; afraid to turn the light on, afraid to leave the light off. Beside me, he slept peacefully.

I was about to violate the sacred "baby rule" and smuggle her into the bed with me, when I heard a voice, tiny and far away.

"Help me!" pierced the darkness. I sat up. "Ayuda me!" followed by the rattle of garbage cans somewhere outside.

"Luie," I whispered, "Luie, wake up. There's something going on." He sprang straight up in the bed, rigid and bleary-eyed, his fists ready for attack. Safety, to Lou, meant always being ready to kill somebody. He reached under the mattress. "No." I put my hand on his. "It's outside. Listen, there it is again." The voice, old and feeble, was a little louder now.

"Help me, Dios, por favor!" again punctuated by the rattle of cans.

Lou picked the "night shoe" from the bedpost and tossed it into the middle of the floor. A few tiny feet scattered.

I followed him to the window to look out onto the cement courtyard that lay between the legs of the 'U' shaped building where the garbage cans were kept, but onto which most tenants simply threw their garbage from the windows.

Toward the front of the 'U', two young guys wearing black "do rags" on their heads were attempting to stuff a skinny little man of about sixty into a trash can.

I followed Lou through the apartment to the kitchen window for a better look. I tried to balance my walk—heavy enough to frighten rats, but not heavy enough to be heard outside.

Lou stood in the corner, out of view, like a spy. I crouched and leaned onto the sill. A bug crawled onto my hand and, as if sensing that it had made a wrong turn, began to move faster up my arm. I had long since given up trying to kill the roaches. It was impossible. There were always more. Instead, I cupped my hand to avoid smearing the thing down my arm and in one wiping move, scooped it up and threw it full force against the wall. It wasn't dead, but I got a great deal of satisfaction in the "thwack" that it made on impact.

Three stories below, the security light spot-lighted the skinny man trying desperately to re-main outside of a garbage can. He looked ridicu-lous in orange-checked polyester bell bottoms and a black net T shirt. A silver-haired and filthy old clown with blood on his face. He moved slowly, lurching and grabbing for the wallet held just out of his reach by one of the boys.

The other boy had the old man around the waist and was trying to turn him, yet again, up-side down. "I don't got no dinero, please," he groaned as, head first, into the can he went. It tipped over. Outside the can, orange and white checks squirmed aimlessly. Inside, a voice pleaded in muffled Spanglish.

The boy with the wallet dropped it and pro-duced a knife from his belt. He smiled at his partner who reached once again for the old toy.

I reached beside me onto the counter for what-ever was there. It was a jar of Welch's grape jelly. "Get outta here, ya scum!" I screamed as I hurled the jar out the window onto the cement below. I held my breath and stepped quickly out of view. Both boys bolted and flew from the courtyard without looking back.

The old guy crawled backward out of the can. He strained his neck and squinted up at silent, blind windows. He struggled to a standing position, a palm on his hip for support. He shook his head slowly, and, talking quietly to himself, began warily gathering the contents of his wallet.

I exhaled. Lou stepped out of the corner, his face a shadowed stone of hatred.

"You stupid, fucking nosey-ass bitch," he said evenly through clenched teeth.

"What?" I backed away from the message flashing in his eyes. "What did I do?"

"How many times do I gotta tell you to mind your fucking business?" His fists opened and closed, opened and closed rhythmically.

"They didn't see me, Lou. They didn't even look up here." Lou kept coming.

"You always gotta show how stupid you are, don't you?" He pushed me. I stumbled backwards out of the kitchen and tripped over the iron pole that stretched across the small entryway—the police lock he'd said would keep me safe.

I fell to the floor. "But they were gonna cut him, Lou!" His eyes wouldn't see me.

"You know what they'll do to you?" he snarled, enraged.

I closed my eyes and hid behind my arms. I tasted the blood more than felt the blows. The side of my head hit the floor.

Finally, he let go of my throat. "You better hope nobody saw your nosey-ass!" He slapped at me as he got to his feet. A few minutes later, on his way from the bathroom, his foot only nudged me. "Get your lazy ass up from there, stupid! Wash your face!"

I didn't want to get up, or move, or open my eyes — ever.

"Can't you hear your damn baby crying? Fucking unfit mother," he mumbled, and walked away, toward the bedroom, "You make me sick!"

My battered face in the bathroom mirror made *me* sick too. A roach crawled across my reflection to pause on the bridge of my swollen and bloody nose.

"Fucking bugs!" I extended a cupped hand toward the vile thing, catching an accidental glimpse of myself in the process. I froze. The face in the mirror looked a lot like the face that had stepped out of the kitchen corner — hateful and stoney. I withdrew my hand in disgust, and stared at the roach. I fancied that it stared back. I craved the satisfying "thwack" of its body against a wall.

The roach, never having intended to represent my miserable status, just sat there, ignorant of itself and of me, an unwitting party to the mockery.

I filled my hands with cool water and splashed my face. The roach didn't move.

We're all the same, I thought, looking at the mirror. Some of us, like the old clown out the window, taunt hopeless young men with glimpses of their future, and some of us remind frightened young husbands of their inadequacies. None of us mean to. I grabbed a can from the shelf, and removed the lid.

The previous thirty minutes replayed in my head; "Thwack!" against the kitchen wall. "Thwack!" into a trash can, "Thwack!" over a police lock. They were crisp, alleviating thwacks. Satisfaction guaranteed.

"You're a roach," I told the mirror, as I doused it in insecticide. "That's all, just a bug."

The tiny creature fell into the sink and I washed it down the drain. The face in the mirror only rippled, staring blankly from behind a wash of bug spray. I turned out the light.

He was asleep by the time I tiptoed back to the bedroom. Marie was asleep a few minutes after. But me, I lay awake in the darkness of the small apartment, and listened as playful rodents scurried across mangled linoleum.

7

Drawing Lines — Choosing Sides

I DIDN'T PARTICULARLY like Elizabeth. She was my neighbor across the hall and we traveled together to avoid the dangers of the subway. Today, I sat in the end seat along the wall in the Bushwick-Aberdeen station, wishing the train would hurry. Some days, like today, I wondered, as Elizabeth droned on and on about her hair, just what was the worst that could happen to me traveling alone.

She was speaking into her compact mirror, and I was ignoring her, when three figures sprang out of nowhere to stand before us.

"This is a stick-up," the guy directly in front of me recited from an old movie. "If you move, I'll blow your head off." A gun rose, seemingly of its own accord, and pointed at my face.

The blood in my body raced toward my feet. When my mouth fell open, the barrel of the gun immediately poked inside. The metal made my mouth water. From my vantage point, it was hard to tell whether the guy held the gun, or vice-versa. They were joined. I stared, cross-eyed, at the connection, unable to look away, for a very long time.

"Where's your money?" he asked me with an eerie calm. I hadn't noticed the others rummaging our purses, but saw now in my peripheral vision, the contents dumped on the platform. My eyes went up his arm as far as his chest and then back to the gun. He pulled it away, and, still pointing it at me, repeated the question.

"I don't have any," I answered in a voice that was equally calm.

He squatted in front of me. His gun hand hung over his thigh, pointed at nothing. His other hand started at my ankle and crawled up my pant leg — a jewelry check.

I looked at Elizabeth. She was way ahead of me with the attention of two guys. She'd been through the jewelry check already and stood, now, against the wall, the subject of a pat-down search.

"C'mon Darryl," one of the searchers hurried my guy. "Move it!"

Darryl half-heartedly checked for jewelry, staring at the floor the whole time. He finished with my first leg, and looked up at me. I noticed, then, just how young he was. I wondered if his mother knew what he was doing. I had an urge to ask him. I didn't. I didn't speak at all. I just looked at him the best I could.

He looked away from me without checking my other leg, and stood up. "OK," he said, and motioned with the gun. "Get up." I stood against the wall as he patted me down. He paused at my left front pocket and I held my breath. "She ain't got nothing," he reported finally. "Let's go."

They were at least thirty foot away, down on the tracks and entering the tunnel, when Elizabeth screamed. I watched them run until they disappeared into the darkness.

The police thought we might be able to catch them in one of the adjoining stations. "It's not every day we get something this fresh."

Elizabeth wasn't up to it. She'd lost a lot of irreplaceable jewelry. Gifts from a friend.

I went.

We didn't find them at the Wilson Avenue station. And they were not at the Broadway-East New York station. We were headed home when I saw them.

"There they are!" I pointed frantically at a light pole on Eastern Avenue.

"Which one had the gun?" the driver demanded, swerving to the curb.

"The one in beige."

The boys moved away from each other when the car stopped. When they saw me in the back seat the chase was on. They ran in three different directions, each seeming to know exactly where to go. Did robbers plan ahead for just such occasions?

Both officers concentrated on the one in beige, Darryl. He ran a short distance, and leapt up on a chain-link fence. They pulled him down easily and walked him the half block to where I was. One stood on the sidewalk, talking to Darryl, while the other radioed for a transport vehicle. When he was inside it, they let me out of their car.

I walked over to the transport car and looked inside. Darryl didn't look at me. He faced me when they told him to, but he didn't look at me. I wasn't sure I wanted him to.

"It's him," I confirmed.

"Are you sure?"

"Absolutely." My voice shook.

He was sixteen years old, and admitted he had robbed us. Elizabeth, who'd joined us at the precinct, hoped he would rot in Hell, and wondered, had they found her jewelry on him? No, but they had found the gun.

"You're lucky it wasn't worse," the officer in charge told us.

I told the man that I thought maybe Darryl had tried to give me a break.

"What're you talking about?" He seemed to become suspicious.

His eyes said I was stupid. "Well, it's just that I've got something . . ." I reached into my left front pocket ". . . and I think he knew I had it."

"Don't kid yourself, sister." He shook his head and snickered. "If that kid had known you had something, you wouldn't have it now. Count yourself lucky he missed it, is all."

He went on to tell me what he knew about "those people."

"It's not enough that they rip off the system for welfare and food stamps, they gotta supplement that by ripping off individuals for everything they got. You pay twice. Once with your taxes, and again when your purse is snatched."

He said a lot more, but I didn't hear him. I was thinking about Darryl, about these people and those people, about drawing up lines and choosing sides. I was confused.

Feeling suddenly guilty, I shoved my food stamps back into my pocket lest anyone see them, and wondered if I had done the right thing, after all.

I was developing a better understanding of life in New York and life in general . . . learning what to expect out of the city. I couldn't say the same about my understanding of Lou. He never failed to shock me, to go further than I could have guessed he'd go. I couldn't anticipate Lou. He wasn't above doing the unthinkable.

8

Whose Monster Is This?

IT WAS NO use arguing about it. He had seen a battery charger in a newspaper flyer yesterday, and he wanted it. He was going to play basketball now, he said, and I was to have the battery charger waiting for him when he got back.

No use reminding him that we didn't have a battery to charge, or a car to put a battery in. It didn't matter. Neither did it matter that the only money we had was the dollar and fifteen cents he was taking with him "for a soda after the game." It was no joke. I knew all too well how serious it was. It had happened before — with the basketball, the sneakers, the spa membership, hand tools, and the workout equipment.

"You understand me?" He asked. "You see which one it is?" He waved the flyer at me.

I nodded, feeling the sick feeling at the top of my stomach.

"Don't get me the wrong one. I don't feel like fighting." The door closed between us.

That sick feeling got worse as the day wore on. It wasn't just that he would hit me today — that I could stand. It was the impending sense of worthlessness I couldn't take. For the next few days, whenever he looked at me he would remind me, with disgust, just how useless I was. Every meal I served would be garbage; every channel change of the TV would be wrong; every bath I ran would be too hot or too cold; the foot rubs and head rubs and back rubs I gave him wouldn't feel right; I'd be "no good for nothing." A condition that wouldn't cause me any real damage, but would bring countless slaps to my head and kicks to my backside. I looked at the picture of the battery charger in the flyer. I hated it. I hated the store that sold it. I hated the flyer. I hated the newspaper for having the flyer in it.

I made the ususal rice and beans for dinner. Then, hoping that something extra would put Lou in a better mood, I asked Señor Vasquez, at the bodega on Bushwick Ave, for credit. "Just until the first," I promised. He let me get a couple of pork chops, an avocado, and a soda.

Lou didn't speak when he came in. He walked into the living room, stepped over the kids watching TV on the floor, changed the channel to baseball, and plopped down on the couch. "I'm hungry." He said it matter-of-factly, without looking away from the set.

Valerie and Marie stood up and went, as invisibly as possible, to their room. Little Luis didn't have a room; he stayed where he was and pretended to watch the ballgame. I pushed the buggy that was Sarah's bed into a corner of the kitchen, where it was less likely to be knocked over, and where she was less likely to be awakened.

He said nothing when I handed him his plate. I moved away quickly, not wanting the sight of me to upset him.

I turned off the bath water and sat on the side of the tub. Waiting to get hit was worse than getting hit. I trembled.

"Let me see the charger." His voice finally came from the living room.

I didn't answer. I heard the creak of the couch, the clank of his plate, his footsteps through the kitchen.

"Well?" He asked. "Where is it?" He stood at the bathroom door.

"I don't have it." I put my head down and prepared for the first blow.

With his right hand, he grabbed my hair and pulled me up and out of the bathroom. The front door was right next to the bathroom, and with his left hand he unlocked and opened it. He let go of my hair and pushed me. I fell out onto the hallway floor on all fours. The door closed and locked behind me. I stayed as I was for a minute, trying to realize what had happened. I wasn't hurt, but I hadn't a clue as to why not, or as to what I should do now. I imagined the other residents of the third floor peering out through peepholes at me, wondering. I didn't want to stand and give them a better look. I half rolled into a sitting position, and scooted back toward my apartment. I hugged my knees up in front of me and lay my head against the door. I listened for whatever might be going on in there. After about twenty minutes all I knew for sure was that

New York was leading Detroit by two at the top of the seventh.

I knocked softly, afraid that he'd answer, more afraid that he wouldn't. He didn't. I tried again, a little louder. Inside, Phil Rizzuto announced the game a little louder. Lou wasn't going to let me in.

It was dark by the time I went downstairs. I folded my bare arms against the chilly wind, and stepped outside. With no idea of where to go, I hurried across the street, into the train station. I asked the woman in the token booth for credit. "Just until the first," I promised. She let me use the gate instead of the turnstyle.

On the train, I struggled to think of someplace to go. A group of teenage boys laughing and pointing reminded me that I was wearing house slippers. I felt sick. I didn't need to be someplace else. Where I needed to be was inside my own home. Sarah was probably awake by now. I put my head down and cried.

I was reluctant to answer when the transit cop asked me if I needed some help. I was nervous. I'd never reported Lou to the police before. I hadn't wanted to get him in trouble. I didn't want people to think badly of him. I'd never admitted to anyone that he hit me. This was different.

"I guess so," I whispered finally.

When I walked back into the apartment building an hour or so later, two police officers from the eighty-third precinct walked in with me. I was no less nervous. The ride over, in the police car, had been torturous. What if Lou still wouldn't open the door? What if he did? What then? The officers had said they weren't allowed to remove Lou from the premises.

"It's on the third floor," I said, and started up the stairs.

As we rounded the landing and came in sight of the apartment, the door flew open. Lou shoved Marie out in front of him. She wasn't crying. She looked dazed. She didn't struggle. He held onto her with his left hand. I saw the paring knife in his right. He said nothing. Both officers froze. Leather squeaked behind me. A holster unsnapped.

"She better get outta here," Lou growled, nodding at me. "Right now!" Neither officer moved.

"That might be a good idea," the officer behind me said, in an unusually even voice. "Why don't you wait for us downstairs?"

I looked at the officer next to me. He nodded without looking at me. His eyes were glued on my husband. I stepped down backwards so as to keep looking at Marie. She didn't look frightened. She looked something else. I didn't know what it was.

"You know, Buddy, you're not in any trouble," the second officer said.

From the landing I could no longer see Marie. I turned and ran. I stumbled down to the second floor. I wanted to stop there and listen, but no. They'd told me to wait downstairs; that's what I'd do. If I did what they told me, everything would have to be all right.

I stood for an eternity at the front door, praying and shaking and waiting. Finally one of the officers yelled for me to "Come on up."

The hallway was empty. Little Luis stood alone in the doorway where Marie had been earlier. He was obviously frightened. I patted his back as I brushed by him into the apartment. I'd comfort him later.

I threw a few things into a bag, gathered the kids together, and collected their shoes and socks. They could put them on in the car. Lou sat on the couch and watched the TV the whole time.

In the car, one of the officers suggested that I go home to my mother. It seemed like a good idea. My mother-in-law had always said that she loved me like a daughter. I gave them her address.

"We couldn't arrest him, you know," he said, without being asked.

"He never really threatened anybody with the knife," the other one said, speaking into the rear-view mirror at me. "Hell, for all we knew, he might've been peeling potatoes when we got there."

"Yeah. He would have to have threatened us," the first officer agreed. "I wish he had."

No one spoke during the rest of the trip.

I sensed, immediately, that my mother-in-law was not happy to see us. If we hadn't needed her help so desperately, I wouldn't have told her what had happened. She didn't look at me, but adjusted and re-adjusted the rollers in her hair as I spoke. When I was done, I didn't know what she thought. She didn't say. She offered neither help nor advice. Why had I thought I could come here? I wondered.

I asked her, straight out, if we could spend the rest of the night here. I assured her that we had someplace else to go at daylight. She didn't answer.

It was after midnight, and I was about to beg when the phone rang. From her end of the conversation I could tell that it was Lou's cousin, Nelson. Poor Lou had tried to kill himself. Slit his wrists. No, she needn't come. He was all right now. In fact, he was home from the hospital already. Did she know that I had left him?

I was stunned. How had Lou known that I would come here? I hadn't known it, for sure, myself.

She let the receiver drop and grabbed me by my shoulders. Her face was filled with hatred as she shook me and sobbed. *"Tu! Mira que hiciste a mi hijo!"*

And of all the things that happened that day, that was the thing that I thought about through the entire train ride home. "You!" she'd screamed as she shook me back and forth. "Look what you've done to my son!"

I suppose this is when I began thinking about monsters, the monsters we become and the monsters we create; the responsibilities we have as human beings, to ourselves and to each other.

Did I, by allowing him to do what he did to me, contribute to his moral decline? What about his mother — by not rejecting his behavior as bad, did she encourage it?

I couldn't begin to answer such questions at that time. I put them aside.

They were questions, however, I would have cause to pick up again, later.

Meanwhile, I was discovering just how shallow Lou really was, and how cruel he could be. It was at this time I began to lose Sarah.

9

Sarah — It Begins

THE ABANDONMENT OF Sarah wasn't a single event so much as it was a process. Although it's difficult to pinpoint exactly when the process was complete, I know when it began.

She was born without complication, beautiful and healthy. I cried. I knew that her father would not be happy. I had practically promised him a boy.

He'd insisted that I could predict the sex of our unborn baby. His mother always had. "Just *feel* it," he instructed impatiently. Finally, knowing what he wanted to hear, I pretended a gut feeling: boy. The only gut feeling I really had was a fear of what might happen if I said "girl."

And now here she was, after all these months — a girl.

I pretended to share his disappointment. Maybe he'd feel better if we were in this together.

I didn't mind not having visitors at the hospital. I enjoyed having Sarah to myself, secretly not caring at all that she was a girl.

On the day that my landlord, Julio, came in his old station wagon and brought Sarah and me home, Lou suggested that we give our daughter to his mother. I hid the shock, but refused, saying simply that it wouldn't be right. I didn't tell him that I didn't want to. He thought about it all the time. He came up with more reasons why it was right, and more ways to give her away without looking bad. We could say that Maria had taken her without permission, and that it would take time to get her back; or that a psychiatrist had said it was the only thing that would save Maria from depression and suicide. The suggestions grew more and more ludicrous, and after a few months, I had to confess that I wanted Sarah.

He acted betrayed. He found ways to punish me for having her; no disposable diapers, he said, and absolutely no night noises. He refused to keep her while I shopped for groceries, or went to the doctor. I wondered why he couldn't see what a nice baby she was.

As far as Lou was concerned, pregnancy was like sex; neither required a wife's consent, and both demanded her cooperation. Sarah was seven months old when I became pregnant again. I was terrified that it was another girl, but claimed, for what it was worth, to "feel" that it was a boy. Sarah was nine months old when I developed the condition that would hospitalize me frequently in the months to come.

Julio's wife came up and got her the first time; a first-floor neighbor kept her the second. By the third hospital stay, I'd run out of acquaintances willing to babysit, and Maria came for Sarah.

Lou and his mother agreed, while I was in the hospital, that the distance between Brooklyn and the Bronx was too great for her to make repeated trips; she would keep Sarah until I was through this, until I'd had the new baby. I returned from the hospital to find not a trace of Sarah in the apartment. "It's just for a few months," I told myself. It would be all right.

On a Thursday, Vanessa was born — another blessing of perfection.

Lou was furious. Security guards put him out of the hospital when he threatened me. He swung at me as they pulled him away, striking me once in the chest. I don't know what they did with him, but he was back that night. He stood outside on the sidewalk and yelled up at my window. He said that he was not going back home — ever. And that he was leaving the kids there alone. I claimed an emergency at home and signed myself out, leaving Vanessa in the nursery.

If Lou was still angry when I met him outside the hospital, I didn't know it. He talked, without threatening me, all the way home. I wasn't sure what to think.

It continued at the apartment. "Show Mommie what I showed you how to do," he encouraged Luis, in some bizarre 'caring father' tone. Luis nervously turned handsprings in the middle of the living room. "See? I told you you could do it," Lou cooed. Some of the sweetness fell from his tone, though, as he added, "If you stopped being a crybaby about it."

He didn't mention the baby once. I didn't either. I didn't dare.

Marie called me awake on Saturday morning.

"Where's your father?" I asked.

"Softball," she answered. "He told me to tell you." She stared at me. "What happened to the baby, Mommie?"

"Nothing, Marie." I smiled. "She's fine — and beautiful. She looks like you."

"Poppy said she was dead."

He was playing basketball when I brought Vanessa home. He came in red-faced and sweaty, with a ball under his arm, and headed into the living room. "Man," he bragged, "you shoulda seen us. We beat the shit outta . . ." I braced myself. The baby was on the couch.

"What the fuck is this?" he demanded. "Bitch, what did you do?"

"It's Vanessa, Lou. You didn't really think I was going to . . ."

I shut up when he dropped the ball and raised his hand as though to hit me, but I knew that he wouldn't. There was no anger in his eyes. There was resignation, intense disappointment, but not anger. Not anymore. I thought for a second that he might cry. He went quietly into the bathroom and ran his own bath. He ate supper in silence, and went into our bedroom.

He was kneeling on the window cushion with his elbows on the sill looking up at the sky when I went in at about ten.

"Aren't you going out?" I asked.

He looked down at his friends gathered beneath the streetlight in front of Chino's. "I don't want her," he said, ever so softly, and without looking away from the guys. He sounded confused, sorry.

"I know," I answered, hating him for sounding soft, for expecting me to understand.

"I could be a good father to the ones we got here, and my mom's already said she'd take . . ."

"No," I said, too quickly, too surely.

I felt the mood change as we sat in silence.

He shouted out the window. "Yo! Orlando!"

Everyone looked up and waved. *"Venga!"*

He stood up. "Don't bring her around me." He sounded a little more like himself. "I don't want her in my room," he warned. "I'm telling you, don't put her where I can see her — ever."

"All right," I replied easily, feeling better about hating him. "All right!" I smiled to myself when he had gone. I had won one. Vanessa would stay.

"What about Sarah?" I asked myself. "One thing at a time," I answered. No sense pressing my luck.

10

Sarah — It's Done

SARAH WAS FIVE years old when her grandmother asked me to sign the papers. "She should start school soon," she explained. I had no right to feel shock at the request, but I did. I had made regular tokens of my continued interest in my daughter, and although I hadn't actually demanded her return, I had planned to; I'd just been very busy. I'd had two more sons in the four years that Sarah had been with her grandmother, and of course, Vanessa. And I was pregnant now. That was a lot of kids, Maria pointed out, that I couldn't afford. I agreed, but giving up Sarah for good was out of the question. It was true that I hardly ever saw the child, but neither did I see any benefit in making it official.

I marvelled at my husband and his mother. These same people who would have died had I ever seriously mentioned birth control, or, God forbid, abortion, saw nothing at all wrong with my just signing my daughter away.

"Hypocrites," I thought. "Damned nervy hypocrites." It reminded me of what my sister had done three years earlier.

My own sister.

The thought still infuriated me. Cindy had invited Marie, who was eight, out to New Mexico for a summer vacation. She'd paid for the entire vacation; all I had to do was to put Marie on a plane. The first letters from Marie said that she was having a great time, that she'd ridden a horse, and that she had a bike to use for the whole summer. "I love you. I'll write more later," closed every letter.

At some point during that summer, my sister decided that I had too many kids to take care of, and that since she didn't have any daughters of her own, she'd do us all a favor and just keep Marie. The letters stopped after that. I'm sure that Cindy's intentions were good, but I missed my daughter.

Getting Marie home had been a major struggle. For one full year, I alternated between threats and pleas to my sister. It completely alienated us. She finally agreed to put Marie on a plane if I could come up with the fare. I borrowed from Sal at the window-glass store on Myrtle Avenue. Marie arrived at LaGuardia just days before her ninth birthday. I had her birthday party at the game room.

And now, two years later, she stood with me in her grandmother's living room in the Bronx. She was my support. I had decided to deny my mother-in-law's ridiculous request, and bring Sarah home, just as I had Marie.

There was no agreement to be reached. I knew that Sarah should go; my mother-in-law knew that she should stay. She gave good reasons. Sarah had nice things here, and her own room. She had peace and quiet, and lots of attention.

But I was her mother, I argued. A child belongs with its mother. What kind of mother would willingly sign these papers?

In the midst of our argument, it occurred to someone to ask Sarah what she wanted. She said without hesitation that she wanted to stay. I said that she couldn't know what she wanted because she was only five years old, and because God only knew what garbage her grandmother might have told her about the rest of us. Things were really heating up when Marie spoke.

"Mommie, why does Sarah have to go if she doesn't want to?" I stopped talking and looked at Marie. She sat on the floor, and looked back at me. I calmed myself with deep breaths and tried to explain it to her. I reminded her that she'd been through something like this herself. She, too, had had nice things, and her own room, when she was in New Mexico, hadn't she? And although she didn't have them now, although I couldn't give her those things, it had still been right for her to come home, hadn't it? She didn't answer.

Hadn't the birthday party been wonderful? She'd looked so pretty, and we'd had so much fun. Marie looked away, and I fell silent. I hadn't forgotten what had happened after the party, but I hoped that Marie would have.

I'd come home after they had, having stayed to clean the party mess. I stood outside the apartment door, holding a bouquet of leftover balloons, and listened for a minute. They were watching television. A comedy. I turned the key quietly, grinned a hugely exaggerated grin, and stuck my head in the door. I froze.

Marie was on the floor in the kitchen, all long, skinny arms and legs, knelt mantis-like. I searched her face for the reason. There was no message, no plea for help in the round black eyes that stole a glance at me from behind black strings of freshly snatched-at hair. The colorful birthday ribbon dangled mockingly in the remaining tangle. As she moved back and forth, it slapped against her face and clashed with the bright red slaps already there.

Silently, she licked her finger, pressed it to the floor, and brushed the adhered crumbs off onto a saucer. She repeated the process in quick jerky motions.

"Don't look at me!" her tense little body screamed out in silence. "You'll make him madder."

I didn't grab her up and run back out the door, but tore my gaze away, and stepped past her into the living room. I sat on the couch with Valerie and Luis and, like them, pretended to be as interested as Lou was in the TV program; pretended not to notice what Marie was doing. The balloons sat, ridiculous now, in my lap.

After ten minutes or so, Marie got the sandwich incident cleaned up and joined us in the living room. She seated herself on the footstool next to her father's chair, and stared at the TV like the rest of us. She listened for his cues, and laughed heartily at all the right times. She was right back in the swing of things, as though she'd never been away.

I watched, now, the tortured face of my oldest child, trapped in a memory, in her grandmother's living room.

"Marie . . ." I remembered how desperately I had wanted her home for that birthday. I put my hand on her shoulder.

"Marie." Silent tears streamed down her face.

"She doesn't have to, Marie," I whispered as I stroked her hair. "She doesn't have to go anywhere she doesn't want to go."

That's when it was complete. That's when I knew that Sarah would stay.

It's become second nature, after all these years, to think of Sarah before I go to sleep. Some people pray; I think of Sarah. I try to imagine how big she's gotten or what she looks like now. I feel as if I know. I mean, she and Vanessa looked so much alike — then.

I know the number to call, but for such a long time I wouldn't. Didn't want to speak to my mother-in-law. Didn't want to answer the questions. Didn't want to hear her — period. The longer I went without calling, the less likely it became I ever would.

They call my grandma's house on Christmas and in April, on Sarah's birthday. I know she's fine. I sometimes wish I could call now. But what would I say? How would I explain all the time I didn't call?

I wonder all the time, though, what does she think of me? Does she feel abandoned? Does she ever cry and wonder why her mommie didn't want her?

Maybe I'm just looking for grief. Maybe the child doesn't care at all, doesn't give me a thought. I can see clearly now — old pain is so much easier to see through — how much she always meant to her grandmother. And who knows? Maybe, by now, her grandmother means just as much to her.

I hope so.

We'd lived in Brooklyn since just after Luis, our third child, was born, and during the last six years I'd hated making the trip to the Bronx. I always took too long. Always got screamed at, at the very least. I had to go, though; his mother was the only person who would lend him any money.

11

Getting Away With Murder

I WAS GOING to be late. The sun was sinking behind the projects on Southern Boulevard as I hurried Valerie and Luis ahead of me down Fox Street. Lou was going to be pissed.

We caught the Number Six at 149th St. The clock in the station read seven-fifteen. He was really going to be pissed.

"Where the fuck have you been?" he demanded as soon as I opened the door.

"At your mother's." I put my head down.

"Don't gimme that shit!" He said, obviously in no mood for any of my "dumb bitch" excuses.

"I couldn't get away, Lou. She kept talking and . . ."

A bright flash filled my head as his fist inter-rupted me. Experience told me there was no use running, but instinct made me turn back toward the door. He grabbed my shirt. It held together long enough for him to get a better hold on me. If he spoke words, I didn't understand them. His voice was all snarls and growls.

Once Lou got started, it was hard to say when it would be enough — when he would stop. Some-times his rage was short lived and other times he just couldn't get enough. This was going to be one of those "other times."

He didn't stop when blood flew from my lips, or when I screamed that my finger was broken. He didn't stop when my eye swelled shut, or when, begging for mercy, I tried to crawl under the bed.

Finally, when I could no longer tell where I was in the apartment, and when I no longer cared whether or not he killed me, it was enough. He dragged me into the living room, screaming for Valerie and Luis to "Get in here and see this!" He ordered them onto the couch, and pulled me up into a standing position in front of them. He stood behind me. His left arm under my chin helped me to stand. His right hand pressed a blade to my neck, just behind my ear. The sweat on my neck belonged to both of us. His chest grew and shrank against my shoulder blades and his breath blew through my hair.

Spittle sprayed the side of my face as he screamed at them. "You weren't at Grandma's were you?!" His arm tightened beneath my chin. His hand jerked my face to the side, to afford them a better view. "I'll kill her if you lie." He spoke a little more calmly now. "Where — were — you?"

Valerie was frozen on the sofa, her hands glued to her head. Her mouth was open far too wide for words and made little squeaking sounds instead. Luis bounced frantically on his knees, his hands clasped in front of him, begging, "No Poppy, no poppy, no, no, oh god no . . ."

I closed my eyes, and prayed the prayers of the damned: "Forgive me," I whispered. "Take me to Heaven. Watch over my kids . . ." On and on I mumbled, ". . . in the name of the father, the son . . ." until finally he cut me.

Blood trickled down my neck. Valerie fell off the couch. Luis buried his face in the cushions and screamed. Lou let go of me. I fell onto my hands and knees. Suddenly everything was quiet.

He hadn't cut me enough to hurt me, only enough to draw blood. I kept my face down. If he saw me looking at the kids, he'd swear we were "ganging up" on him.

After a few seconds, I heard the blade close. "Lying Motherfuckers!!" He kicked the wall a few times on his way out, but he didn't touch me again. When the door slammed behind him I let myself collapse. They rushed to me. Little fingers stroked my head, and a wet washcloth covered my face. I think it helped them to be able to help me.

He returned a little after one, carrying a pizza and a meatball hero, ignoring the rice and beans I'd kept warm for him. I knew what was expected of me; I sat at the table with him. He looked at my face and shook his head. I didn't flinch when he reached for me. He tilted my head a little so he could see the tiny knick he'd made on my neck.

"I swear to God," he said as he lifted the hero to his mouth. "You're gonna make me kill you some-day."

It was after two when he called me into the living room. He was sitting on the couch with one of the guns from the closet in his hands. "My kids are gonna hate me. You know that?" He had a strange look on his face. I didn't say anything. "I'm talkin' to you! Why don't you fuckin' answer me?"

"I'm sorry, Lou." I was shaking.

"If I was your dad wouldn't you hate me?"

"No," I lied, trying not to look at the gun.

He looked at me for a moment, disgusted. "It don't matter." He shrugged. "None of you is gonna hate me after tonight."

My heart raced. "What do you mean?"

"You're going to do us all a favor."

He instructed me slowly, carefully. I was to wait until he was asleep. I would make sure by tickling his foot. Then I would press the gun to his head. He showed me the spot on his temple. "Right here," he said. "Angle it back just a little, like this." He didn't think the broken finger on my right hand would be a problem. I could do it left-handed. The important thing was to keep the end of the barrel steady against his head.

He placed the gun on the end table, and faced me. Speaking to my very soul, he said, "If you don't do this, you're going to be sorry. I'm warning you." His eyes belied the calmness in his voice. "I better not wake up." With that, he spread out on the couch, turned his back to me, and closed his eyes.

I don't know how long I sat staring at the thing. He was asleep when I finally picked it up. It was a .38-caliber revolver that looked as though someone had put it together out of parts. He'd never liked this gun. Wouldn't carry it. Said it was unreliable. It struck me as incredibly funny that he would choose this gun to die by.

I deliberated for hours over his right to live, or to die; about whether my duty was to kill him, or to not kill him; about what might happen to me if I did, and what might happen if I didn't; about what the kids would think.

At one point, he stirred on the couch. I thrust the gun in the direction of his head, deciding in an instant to pump all six bullets into his face. But he only rolled over without waking. After a few minutes my heartbeat slowed to normal and I went back to my thoughts.

By six-twenty, I still didn't know if he should live or die. Or how to figure it out. I put the gun in the closet and went to bed.

At nine-thirty, Lou woke up, and in so doing assumed all was well, that he'd been forgiven, and that his wife loved him very much.

12

Time to Stop Pretending

IT WAS A typical morning after. I snuck out of bed, turned the alarm off an hour before it was due to ring, and stood in front of the mirror. My eye looked pretty good in the dim light of the bedroom. "It should be blacker than that," I thought. I tiptoed out of the bedroom. "It sure as hell hurts worse than that."

The bathroom mirror better reflected how I felt. My left eye was bright red where it should have been white. A deep purple surrounded it and faded out across the bridge of my nose. A decidedly lighter purple—almost blue—ran down my jaw. Dried blood decorated the corner of my mouth. Looking at it hurt my eyeball. I held a folded washcloth over it and continued to look with my other eye. It hurt to open my mouth wide. I had bitten my tongue and it was in bad shape. What I could see of my teeth seemed to be all right. Could have been worse, I supposed. I turned out the bathroom light.

I couldn't put a name to the strange fear that nagged me as I started breakfast. I wasn't really scared of him this morning; I was pretty sure he'd had enough last night. An absurd thought crossed my mind: perhaps it was myself that frightened me. I swallowed the notion and immediately a spring began to wind in my chest.

Time got away from me. I was ten minutes late waking him.

"Bitch!" He called from the bathroom. "Stupid fucking bitch!"

The spring in my chest wound tighter.

"She must like getting hit," he said, as if to himself. "Why else she's gonna make me do this?" He stopped talking and I heard him brushing his teeth. After a minute or two he stepped out of the bathroom, his teeth clamped around the toothbrush. The muttered "Bitch!" didn't sound quite right. I instinctively dodged the tube of toothpaste, and the spring in my chest wound tighter.

He stepped back into the bathroom. He spat and his voice started again, only now it just sounded like "Blah-blah." My chest began to hurt. I bent to pick up the toothpaste tube, and a deodorant stick whizzed by me, punctuating the blah-blah and crashing into the oven door. I clenched my teeth, and ran my fingers through my hair. Swallowing a scream, I began wiping toothpaste off the cabinet. A bottle of after-shave hit my elbow. It did more than just send a shock of pain all the way to my shoulder; it released something inside me. Something frightening, something wonderful. I dropped the dishrag and walked toward the living room. He threw a can of spray disinfectant. Somewhere in me, I knew that it hit my head. I knew, but it didn't hurt, and I didn't care.

He stomped after me, the blah-blah getting louder. I didn't care. His hairbrush broke when it hit my shoulder. My shoulder didn't care. He grabbed my hair. I sat down on the floor, and stared at the side of the old couch that his aunt had given us. I was aware of the fact that he slapped me at one point, but it was not nearly as important as the fascinating patterns in the upholstery of this couch. I'd never seen anything as beautiful. I reached out to touch it. It was strange. I could touch it, but I couldn't feel it. The blah-blah faded away.

"Mommie," Marie's voice sounded funny, far away. I looked up and was surprised to see her hand on my shoulder — I hadn't felt her touching me. "It's all right." She said, looking at me as if she didn't really think so. "He's gone."

I came to be in the bathroom. The wonderful and frightening thing was not gone. I had a dreamy, half-here feeling about me. I liked it. Valerie's voice on the other side of the door, I did not like. I felt strangely inhibited by it.

"Mommie, please. Are you O.K.?" She knocked softly as she spoke.

I ignored her and peered into the mirror. Finally Valerie faded and I was alone. I was looking in the mirror, kind of playing with my hair when the answer came to me. I suddenly knew. I knew I didn't have to keep the misery going; that it would be finished whenever I wanted. I felt, suddenly, the power to stop it all. "Whew!" I breathed. "I don't have to do this anymore." I almost giggled as I told the mirror, "I quit."

They came running when I opened the bathroom door, stopping just short of touching me.

They looked at each other, questioning. I grabbed them up, one by one, without feeling them. I hugged them too hard for too long, wondering if I would miss them where I was going. I whispered eerily into their ears about the time to stop pretending. I was at Marie's ear when the familiarity of the words struck me. A scene from another time flashed in my head. I recognized it immediately. A chill sped up my back, raised the hairs on my neck, and brought throbbing life to a painful knot that the spray can had raised on my head. Within seconds everything hurt again. I held Marie at arm's length and examined her face, half expecting to see someone else. Myself, maybe.

"What?" She cried. "Mommie, you're scaring me." I was scaring myself. I raced to the bathroom mirror, afraid to look. I couldn't explain the relief I felt when I saw my own reflection.

I sat on the side of the tub and struggled to understand. Had I really been prepared to do that? I felt everything at once. Foolish, guilty and crazy. Definitely crazy. How could I have so horribly confused destiny and memory? I felt relief and shame. Shame not that my mother had killed herself, but that, for all my adult life, I had, in some weird memorial tribute, been doing the same.

"I'm sorry," I whispered. Tears slid down my face. Twenty-years-late tears; tears for her pain, her life, her death. Tears for my mother.

"Mommie?" Marie called through the door.

"Just a minute," I answered. For the first time in my adult life I didn't think I sounded like somebody else. I stood and dabbed a tissue at my nose and cheeks. "I'm coming." I felt strangely excited. Eager to start my own life, wondering what it would be like. I tucked my mother's life safely into my memory where it belonged, and opened the door.

I'll never understand exactly what it was that made that July day unbearable for me, or why it hadn't happened sooner.

Whatever the reason, I finally had had enough, and after thirteen years of marriage and eight children, I escaped. With nothing. Not even a plan.

We just left — Marie, Valerie, Luis, Vanessa, Juan, Jorgie, Donald, and I.

We hit the streets. . .

13

Win or Lose

GRANDMA'S STRICTEST RULE involved charity. She hated the concept. She attempted a Bible quote: "Them that won't work kayn't eat." She prided herself on having raised two daughters during the depression era. She "never so much as bawreed a dime."

I remember going to the store with Grandma during what she called "bad times." One day in particular stands out. It was between paydays and I had turned my back as she dug the jar out of her bedroom closet. I faced her and watched as she counted out twenty-nine quarters, then faced away again as she returned the sacred jar to its hallowed hiding place somewhere among the mysterious boxes and bags that lined her closet floor, probably next to the Redman tobacco which she somehow thought nobody knew she chewed.

We walked to the store, Grandma using the full six blocks to contemplate every penny of the seven dollars and twenty-five cents she carried in a little flannel bag with the drawstring pulled tight. By the time the automatic doors anticipated our entry, she knew exactly, to the item, what she would buy. All I knew, as I hopped onto and off of the black ribbed pads in an attempt to psych out the automatic doors, was that I would indeed eat tonight. I always did.

Despite all of Grandma's planning, shopping with her took forever. She had to examine and comment on the price of every item in the store. As she checked the dog food on this particular day, I dug into the deepest reserves of my ten-year-old wit. "Are we gettin' a dog, Grandma" I giggled, "or are we gonna eat that ourselves?" I held back hysterical laughter. She slapped me on the back of the head. "Act like you got some sense! People'll think you're serious."

Once in the checkout line, Grandma counted her money again, carefully matching it up with the items in our cart. The line was long. I was bored. My head got slapped twice more, once for almost stepping on a woman in the next line, (Grandma made me stand on the side of the cart after that) and again for doubling over into the cart with an exaggerated sigh of exhaustion. But when I leaned back a minute later and fell off the cart, she didn't even notice. The woman directly ahead of us had stepped to the front of her cart. It was almost her turn to put groceries on the belt. She had taken from her purse some strange bills that looked like play money. Grandma was checking out those bills. She seemed to be matching them up with the items in the woman's cart. I got up from the floor, ducking my head a little. "Sorry Grandma." She didn't hear me; she was moving toward the woman.

"Izzat food stamps?" Grandma asked. I barely heard the woman mumble, "Yeah."

"I know all about those," Grandma began. "Those are my tax dollars, sister, an if you kayn't feed yourself, a grown woman big as you are, an if you wanna live offa my hard work, that's your shame. But by God, you ain't gonna eat better than me!" She began to go through the groceries in the woman's cart, 'suggesting' alternatives to the better cuts of meat, removing the items she didn't approve of. Nobody stopped Grandma. Some people looked away but most just stared. I don't know how the woman felt; she never said a word. Her face, which I could see from my somewhat lower perspective, showed red behind the hair now hanging forward to cover it. She stumbled and nearly fell getting past the woman ahead of her who, in the process of paying the cashier, held up "real" money. The fleeing woman, faster than the automatic door, pushed unsuccessfully against it. In the second or two that she waited for it to swing open, something about her posture gave me chills.

"It ain't fair," Grandma explained on the way home. It didn't matter if the woman was hungry or even if she starved to death, as long as she did so with dignity and didn't ask anybody for anything. "It ain't whether you win or lose, girl, it's how you play the game."

Twenty years later, in a dirty New York subway station, the memory of that day slapped me full on the face. In a rushed decision, I had fled my home and husband for the safety of the streets. In my hurry, I had taken my children and nothing else. We had been "out" for about thirty hours, sleeping on the train, getting off only to use the bathroom, miss the rush hours, or to avoid being seen too frequently by the same transit cop. We ate nothing.

We sat on the station steps, waiting out this particular rush hour, as I explained to three-year-old Juan, once again, why we couldn't "just go home." The approach of evening brought mixed feelings: a break in the heat would be a blessing, but . . . well, things change in New York at night. The streets — and the train stations — get ugly. In the shadow of impending darkness and another sleepless night, my reasons for leaving home seemed rather flat; one fear crushed under the weight of another. At home, one madman with a fiberglass fishing rod or other weapons I was familiar with; out here, a score of madmen wielding God knows what. I opted for the unknown madmen. Open spaces offered at least a chance to run under attack.

Tunnel air has a way of blending heat and odors. My nasal passages had long since swollen shut against the onslaught of the trademark train station combo: body odor, newspaper ink, and urine. Although appalled at the thought of this concoction travelling across my tongue, I forced myself to suck the abomination into my lungs through my mouth. If our location imposed nausea, it also offered comfort: smooth, cold cement steps with thin sandpaper-like strips near the edges, cool tile walls, refreshing against the cheek. Marie, my twelve-year-old, raised her shirt a little, from time to time, to press her back against the tile.

This particular stairwell ran between two levels within the station. Those travelling it were merely passing through. Few people would have considered exiting the subway in this neighborhood. Most were changing trains on their way home from work. They hurried. This was no place to be after dark, when the nocturnal elements of the community above would seep down into the tunnel. I wanted us out of this station. As soon as the crowds thinned out, we would be on a train — any train. I had no idea where we'd go; we'd just *go*.

Right now, Jorgie, my eighteen-month-old, needed changing. I had no more diapers. Marie held the smaller baby while I went to a nearby bathroom to clean Jorgie. Fifteen minutes later, the last pretty thing about me, my undershirt, black with embroidered lace, was wrapped snugly around Jorgie's bottom. With wet paper towels I dabbed at the dirt on his face. He cried almost nonstop. The child was hungry. They were all hungry — not with an almost-dinnertime hunger, but with a painful and frightening emptiness. The madman husband with a fishing rod seemed less and less menacing.

"Tomorrow," I thought out loud to Jorgie, "Tomorrow something will turn up." Of course we couldn't wait until tomorrow, but for the moment, this was better than *home*. We would hold out as long as we could.

"What happened?" I demanded. Marie was rushing up the stairs to meet me.

"Nothing bad," she smiled, looking too tired for a twelve-year-old girl. An exhausted braid ran down her back with more hair out than in. Her face was smudged with what I hoped was only dirt. The legs of her jeans, like my own, showed stiff spots, where overused diapers had leaked. Her light blue T shirt showed dirt and sweat wiped from smaller faces. "Look what I made while you were gone." She held out a hand that made her face look clean. In it was money — a few dollar bills and a lot of change.

"Marie, where did you get that?" Something about this frightened me.

"I didn't do anything, Mom. A man came by, handed me a dollar, and said 'get the baby some milk.' After that everybody that came by handed me something." She laughed. "I guess Donny really made the money."

My mouth fell open. I wanted to slap the child on the back of the head. I looked around at my other children. Juan was climbing over and rolling under the handrail. Luis was sliding down the steps on his stomach. They were filthy. I was devastated. People had mistaken my precious little children for panhandlers.

"Seven dollars and twenty-five cents!" Marie reported cheerfully. Grandma sent me an icy chill from I don't know where. I looked at the money in Marie's hand, the smile on her face.

"Marie," I began, not knowing what I would say. "Marie, we. . . " I bit my lip and stared at her in silence as she waited for me to continue. I wanted to shout at her that we never take things from other people, but she looked so proud. I wanted to slap her on the head and fling the horrid money as far as I could, but they were all so hungry. I wanted to tell her about Grandma's dignity, that it's not whether you win or lose, but how you play the game. I wanted to — maybe I should've, but I didn't. I took the money. I took the money, found a transit cop and asked for help.

I took it because sometimes in this life things turn upside down. Sometimes the rules that you stand on are pulled out from under you. Injured perspectives swell, too big to be cloaked in the ideals that once wrapped them. I took it because sometimes in this stupid game that my grandmother spoke of, things more valuable than your soul are at stake and lives more precious than your own hang in the balance. I took the money because sometimes it really ain't how you play the game; it's whether you win or lose.

14

Meeting Lady Liberty

WE LOOKED AWFUL. No one touched us as we crept up out of the subway at dusk. When a small man in a silk shirt looked up from his paper just in time to miss brushing against me, he gasped and folded the *New York Post* under his arm indignantly. He looked back at us and frowned as he crossed the street, shaking his head in disgust. I locked my eyes straight ahead and did not cry.

The transit cop had scrawled directions to the E.A.U. (emergency assistance unit) on a tiny rip of paper which I held loosely so as not to sweat the ink away. I dropped it as we rounded the corner onto Willoughby Street. I wouldn't need directions.

It was an ugly, stubby little building that just kind of squatted alongside the street, completely outclassed and outcast by the taller, sleeker structures that surrounded it. It was infested with humans. They mulled about it, back to front, side to side, in all shapes and sizes. At one corner crouched three unshaven men of vague age, whispering and gesturing drunkenly. One of them was without a shirt. On the sidewalk not far from them a grey-bearded man lay sleeping, his back against the wall. He wore a grey hat and clutched a grey coat in his arms. The shirtless man rose from the group, and with a shushing finger to his grinning lips, stepped sneakily up to the building, unzipped his pants, and urinated on the wall just above the sleeping man's head. His friends howled encouragement. When the urine shower failed to rouse the grey man, the shirtless one shrugged his shoulders clumsily, and half-heartedly kicked at him. He gave up finally, spitting on the sleeper as he staggered back to his friends. The other fifteen or so people in front of the building didn't seem to notice.

My eight-year-old son, Luis, noticed. He seemed at first mesmerized by the swirling puddle. Then, repulsed, he began to gag, his eyes glued to the stream trickling away from the man's head.

"Don't look!" I ordered. He continued to look and to gag. Valerie joined him after a few seconds, then Marie. It was easy to see where this was going. "Stop it!" I demanded. "Stop it now!"

"Hey, little Sweetie," a raspy voice interrupted. "Tell me something." The woman was round. Her huge breasts pointed at Luis from behind a red acrylic knit top. Bra straps hung, dingy grey, down her black arms. Her hands were on his shoulders. One held a smoking cigarette. I moved closer to my son, grasping his arm at the elbow. "Can you think of something purple for me?" she asked looking into his face.

"No!" He pulled away from the woman, shaking his head fiercely.

She insisted. "You can't think of one single purple thing?"

He shook his head again, but it had worked— the gagging had stopped.

She didn't hear my mumbled thanks. She and her friends had disappeared around the side of the building, taking turns drinking from a two-liter Pepsi bottle as they went.

A skinny man with a star tattooed on his forehead and a vacant look in his eyes opened the door
for us. He was barefoot and had a silly grin on his
face. I nodded my appreciation. He let the door
close on me. Several people snickered.

The room was alive. People and bags were everywhere. Half-walls divided the edges of the
room into little nooks, with six chairs in each. The
center was a jumble of disorder. Here and there a
pair of just-washed underwear hung over the back
of one of the plastic chairs that crowded the place,
blue and yellow, blue and yellow.

"Sign in and take a seat," the woman droned,
not bothering to look up from her crossword
puzzle.

The nook in the farthest corner was occupied by
only two people. Perhaps we could make do with
the remaining four chairs in that section, away
from the center throng.

The old woman who rose to greet us was mute,
but her ready stance and the mace that hung at
her belt told me that we would share this nook
with her only if she didn't mind. I couldn't guess
how old she was. Her hair, pulled back in a rubber band, was long and grey, brittle where it

hung, but oily near the scalp. She looked us over carefully, one at a time, and scratched her head. Large flakes sprinkled her nose and cheeks. She must've liked us. Bits of black decay dotted a pink smile and seasoned the breath that traveled the four feet between us. Her companion was about nineteen. A dried yellow blot stained the front of his light blue pants. He nervously waited for her nod before smiling a welcome.

The odors here were concentrated, stagnant. There was old urine mostly, peppered here and there with fresh urine and laced with body odor. The sinus-inflaming newspaper ink was blessedly absent. I had no idea what the sticky substance was on the wall next to me, or why the floor was slippery in spots. "Don't touch anything," became the rule for the duration, and "think purple" was the game of the day.

No one seemed too bothered by the obvious dirtiness of the dinner bread. And no one mentioned the strange taste of the peanut butter. I think they all felt it. We were closing in. We had lived through the trains. All we had to do now was make it through an application process. How long could that take? We'd soon have someplace to go — beds. It didn't matter how bad the food was, or how dirty the room was, or how crazy the people were, we weren't going back home. We were on our way to freedom. Then two things happened: the loud speaker told us to expect no further shelter placements until eight a.m. Monday, (Midnight marked the beginning of the holiday weekend which, by the way, they hoped we'd enjoy safely) and Vanessa got diarrhea. It was while holding her tired little body over a waste-smeared toilet seat in a stall with no door, shushing her tears of fear and embarrassment, that I realized that some things do matter. I began to doubt our chances.

The mute woman's trumpeted breakfast call woke me with a start and sent an uncomfortable ripple through the sleeping bodies in the room. "Crazy old bag of bones!" someone muttered sleepily. The kids were sprawled across chairs and on the floor all around me. My neck was impossibly stiff from sleeping in the plastic chair all night. My eyes focused on the stack of sandwiches she offered. "Shut the fuck up!" someone shouted from the floor as my new friend walked from one to the other of my children, patting heads and shrieking appraisals of individual appetites.

At four o'clock in the afternoon, I pulled the dime from the watch pocket of my jeans. A dime that I'd kept through it all. A dime that I'd hoped I would never use.

Louie wasn't home. We would have to wait. I couldn't go back without talking to him first. I'd have to let him convince me to return. That way I could bargain. He'd promise to change. I'd pretend to believe him. Things would be all right — for awhile.

I returned to my corner. The old woman squawked at me from her seat. The kids sat on the floor unwrapping Now&Laters she'd given them. She grabbed a filthy bag from beneath her chair and started toward me. She couldn't know how loud or how hard she cackled as she patted Juan's head in passing. She winked at me conspiratorially. I couldn't think of an excuse not to follow her when she motioned for me to.

Once in the bathroom, she reached down into the bag and pulled, from amid the soaps, candies, and various pieces of clothing, several rubber band-bound bundles: sparklers and bottle rockets.

"Unnnh?" She brought them to the mouth of the bag and no further, lest someone else should see. "Unnnh?" she repeated.

"Oh, boy!" I mouthed with exaggerated lip movements. "That's good."

She let out a ripsnorting cackle.

It was after nine when I dragged myself out of the phone booth again, turning the dime over and over in my hand. He still wasn't home.

Out in the parking lot, the display had begun. I took a seat on the asphalt beside my family and watched as one bottle rocket after another zipped over the dumpy little building. The boys giggled and jumped with each one. Valerie laughed, tickled at the old woman's animation. The sound was one I hadn't heard in a long time. It made me feel relaxed, strangely comfortable.

Our hostess picked up a bundle of sparklers and grew serious. She quieted the crowd with a gesture, lit one of the sticks with as much theatrics as possible, and to the delight of the entire audience, struck a near-perfect imitation of the statue. Something happened to me as I looked at her.

She stood there, one arm across her abdomen, the other holding the sparkler high over her head, a ragged and toothless old Miss Liberty poised with dignified satisfaction in the middle of the dirty parking lot beside the refuge, children oohing and ahhing at her feet. The old woman's body made three complete revolutions during the life of that sparkler; I made one.

As she turned, I understood. Her face said more to me than any lips ever had. She told me without words the truth about freedom. That its face isn't lovely and that its voice doesn't float liltingly on sweet breath. She reminded me that freedom does not clean, clothe, feed, or educate, but rather, that it is its own value.

By the time the sparkler died out, I knew that I would never go home. I would never again negotiate for artificial freedoms. I wouldn't make phone calls in the night, or strike deals or be rescued. She had reminded me that real freedom can't be gotten that way.

I stood, drew back my arm and flung the dime into the darkness.

Juan clapped his hands together in excitement as I took the sparkler she offered and held it high. It glimmered and spat against the night sky. Her brash cackle ripped the air — too loud, too hard. I smiled at her.

"Happy Fourth of July," I whispered.

15

Puppies and Things

IT WAS THREE o'clock in the morning on July seventh when a worker at the emergency assistance unit told me about a vacancy at Four Bells, a shelter on the other side of Brooklyn—a space large enough to suit my family. We were off.

The train station was empty but for our family and two other people. A young woman with the fingers torn out of her gloves chatted with herself as she strolled back and forth, pausing now and then to rummage in a trash bin. There was something about her eyes. I couldn't name it exactly; they were oddly set. "I didn't do it," she told herself.

A man leaned against a tile pillar and stared at the girl from behind a newspaper. I got the feeling that this was the only place he was going tonight, and that a train was not what he was waiting for. He had dressed himself to fit in; he stood out. His face was too clean and too soft for the hard burgundy denim that he wore. The words, "Yo! We go!" were written in black magic marker across the back of his jacket. He didn't look like a "we" man. He looked like the kind of loner that the muggers had been avoiding since the Bernie Goetz thing. I guessed him to be about twenty-five. I was certain he was dangerous.

Transit cop shoes clicked confidently somewhere above us. The burgundy weirdo snatched another draw from his cigarette, and snubbed it out just as they appeared on the stairway of the opposite platform.

I stared across the tracks at the cops clicking and whistling their way along the deserted platform. When one of them bent to touch something, I strained to see.

He poked at some trash on the floor—debris that I guessed had been blown about by passing trains and had collected in piles against the wall. Gradually, as he stirred the mess with his stick, I realized there was an order to the piles. I was ashamed that I hadn't noticed them before, and fascinated. They lay where the floor met the wall, covered with whatever cardboard or newspaper their indifferent, unwitting benefactors had donated.

The nightsticks, without malice for now, tapped tired feet and nudged weary bottoms. "C'mon guys. Let's go. Can't stay here." I stared in amazement as the lumps stirred, rose, and finally lumbered off out of sight behind the stairwell. An absurd caravan of upright turtles, their shelters on their backs.

The train doors, struggling to close, bumped and bounced against Valerie as I maneuvered the others onto the train. The girl with the funny-set eyes got on with us. I was glad. I'd wondered what would happen when I was no longer there to shoot menacing looks at the weirdo every time he tried to get her attention with a sneaky "Psssst."

She sat next to me, her knees together and her hands gripping the bench on either side of them. She spoke out, now and again, to no one. "It wasn't me," she announced out of nowhere. "I didn't do it."

I spoke to her finally because I didn't know what else to do. She said that she had run away from home, and that she had new shoes. I looked at the ragged canvas high tops on her feet — men's Converses, way too big. She didn't have to go back, she told me, fidgeting as she spoke. She was a big girl now. She patted the top of her head and smiled at me. I figured her to be about twenty.

I said "Um-hum" because I didn't know what else to say, and looked away.

"I said it wasn't me!" She shouted when I had been dozing for a few minutes. I snapped up straight and jerked my head in her direction. She smiled sweetly, looking as if she hadn't said or heard a thing.

I never actually saw her move closer to me. She just did. And then she was dozing against my arm. I looked at her and remembered a dirty little puppy that had followed me home in the second grade. My mother told me to take it back where I'd found it. I hid it in my room. My sister said the puppy would give me worms, matt my eyes shut, and make my hair fall out. Terrified, I took it back to where I'd found it. I put it down and said good-bye. It wouldn't stay. When I walked, it followed. I stamped my foot at it. "Shoo!" I ordered. "Go away!" But when I walked, it followed. Again I stamped and shooed. It bounced around my feet, wagging its tail. Finally, panicked by the prospect of worms and matted eyes, and not knowing what else to do, I kicked the puppy as hard as I could. It yelped and scrambled to its feet. It cowered and shivered, ears down and tail between its legs. But it stayed then. Only its eyes, big and round and sad, followed me. I felt them on me as I ran.

I looked, now, at the child dozing on my arm. I wondered where she had come from. Somebody must be worried about her. She was just a little girl. I noticed a slight motion within her dark hair and caught my breath. I watched as tiny little aliens poked and weaved, nearly transparent, in and out of the oily strands.

"Oh shit!" My whole body stiffened. She jumped.

"I didn't do it!" Her funny-set eyes sprang open wide with uncertainty.

I wanted to push her. Not just away from me, but down. Onto the floor. I wanted to draw up my knees and shove my feet into her as hard as I could.

"I didn't do it," she repeated.

I clamped my mouth closed, and held my breath. I gathered the length of my hair to the opposite side of my head, and tried to smile as I settled back.

"Please don't let me get headlice," I prayed silently. "Please don't let me get headlice."

Headlice or no, she was with us now, and I couldn't just leave her on the train. I woke her at our stop. But shelters have procedures and policies. She couldn't get in.

"You're kidding!" I knew that the man behind the desk was not.

"I'm sorry." He said, looking as though he really was. "No can do."

I pointed out that she was plainly in need of help, and just as plainly not capable of asking for it.

"Sorry. No." He repeated.

"O.K." I gave up. "It's four-thirty in the morning. What do we have to do?"

"She has to go to the E.A.U. and fill out the same forms you did, and . . ."

"What!?"

"AND we've got a waiting list. A single adult can only be accepted or denied for one night at a time." He looked ashamed.

I imagined her going back and forth to the E.A.U. and through the paperwork every day.

"Sorry," he said one more time.

I told myself not to beg. She stood out on the steps and looked at me. I begged. I explained that I didn't know this girl, that she had just kind of latched onto me in a train station, and that I had reason to think that she couldn't take care of herself.

He looked her up and down and assured me that she could. "She's made it this far," he reasoned.

I said he didn't care.

He said I was free to stay outside with her.

I turned away.

He stood and went to the door.

I heard him telling her about a "friendly" park right down the street.

I told myself not to forget. I wanted to be guilty and outraged all night. It was only a short while before I stretched out across the bed, and forgot.

We woke at lunchtime and showered before we ate. I brought dinner rolls and crackers, stolen from the Four Bells dinner hall, to the park down the street.

She talked as she ate, telling me all over again about running away, and about her new shoes. It occurred to me that maybe she didn't recognize me today. I walked back to the shelter, not sure if it mattered whether she did or not. My shower had made her smell bad.

She smelled even worse the next morning. I sat with her on a ledge while she ate one of the bagels in silence. She put the other one in her pocket. I worried, as I walked back to the shelter, about her silence. "Maybe she doesn't like bagels."

On the third day she wasn't at the park. I waited around for a while but she didn't come, and I had to get back. I asked some of the park "regulars" if they'd seen her. They didn't know who I was talking about. I left the biscuits on the ledge, and started back to the shelter, ashamedly relieved.

She was not behind me. I turned around twice to check. "Her eyes are not following me," I told myself.

Still, I felt them on me as I ran.

16

My Kind of People

THE SHELTER WE were staying in would work in a pinch, the woman at the E.A.U. said when I went back for an extended referral, but it wasn't really for us.

They'd forwarded referrals for me to all the battered-women's shelters. That's where I ought to be, she said. Those places were made especially for people like me. When one of the referrals paid off, I went.

It was after two in the morning when we arrived at the Martinique hotel on West Thirty-second Street, but the desk clerk was waiting for me; the E.A.U. had phoned ahead. As I signed the back of the two-party check they'd given me, I couldn't help noticing it was made out for more money than I'd paid for a month's rent in Brooklyn. The woman at the E.A.U. had said it would cover three days and nights at this hotel. After that, I would need a referral to the welfare office on Fourteenth Street. Not to worry, she said. A caseworker in the hotel would write it up for me.

Our room was on the fourteenth floor. I could look out at Macy's department store. If I stuck my head out the bathroom window and twisted it just right, I could look straight up the Empire State Building.

We had our own bathroom, and our own light switch. I couldn't believe the kick I got out of flipping it off and on again.

The woman at the E.A.U. had said there would be people like me here, but after a week in this place, I hadn't met any such people.

I'd met Carmen, an eighteen-year-old and obvious huffer who was hiding here, not from an abusive husband, but from her father who'd beaten her and her two kids. I'd met Frieda, who regularly had to be stopped from furiously beating her own three kids right here in the shelter. I'd met Anita. I didn't even try to guess where she went or what she did every night when she left her two-year-old son with Carmen and snuck past the guard at the elevator.

I hadn't actually met Lydia, but had found her dead husband's ashes in the "grab room," where extra or donated clothing and miscellaneous items were kept for rummaging through by those who may have arrived less than prepared. The ashes were in what looked like a regular paint can, the kind whose top pries off with a screwdriver. There was a generic-looking label on the can stating his name and the name of a prison upstate. "What's this?" I asked. The can rattled strangely as I shook it. It sounded like little rocks scattered in a can of dirt.

"Ha!" Frieda laughed. "That's Umberto, Lydia's husband. She left him here a few years ago. Nobody takes him out. Everybody thinks this is a good place for him." She laughed again.

I put the can down quickly. "What do you mean?" I asked.

Frieda sighed deeply. "Umberto tried to kill Lydia," she began, obviously bored. "Shot her twice. He went to prison for it, and some kind of way he died there." She rummaged through a box of shirts as she recited. "They sent his ashes to

Lydia's apartment. Her Mom didn't know what to do with them so she brought them here to Lydia."

I thought for a minute. "If her husband was in prison, why was Lydia here?" I was not sure I believed her.

She sucked air through her teeth and said it was a stupid question. "She was hiding out from her boyfriend. He used to beat her up, too."

I looked down at the can. "Oh." I said softly. "What happened to Lydia?"

"I don't know." Frieda shrugged her shoulders, interested now in a sweatshirt she'd pulled from the box. "I only heard the story from the caseworkers. They told us to leave the can here. Hey, they got new stuff in here. Nobody told me."

My caseworker's name was Gloria. She told us in group sessions that she was a battered woman. The experiences she talked about, though, weren't like any I'd ever had. Or anybody else in the place. She talked about not getting to choose a vacation spot, and feeling pressure to join her husband at the cottage on the lake. Robin, the girl in the room next to mine, couldn't relate. She said once, right out in group, that Gloria's stories were bullshit crybaby stuff and that Gloria should keep her mouth shut in our group meetings. Gloria responded with a lecture entitled "What is abuse?" Actually, the lecture made sense. But so had Robin. I didn't know who was right. She said it didn't matter, and that Robin's comments didn't bother her.

I went to her office the following day to get my weekly referral to the welfare office.

I thanked her when she offered to write me an extra referral for clothing.

"Don't thank me," she said. "I like doing things for you. You're not like these other people."

I was standing to leave when she continued nastily, "Not like that twirpy little bitch, Robin." I didn't say anything and she went on. "She thinks we don't know she's seeing her husband while she's here."

"She is?" I asked, not sure I really cared.

"Hell yeah, she is!" she waved her hand furiously. "He picks her up right out front. She's giving him the Goddamn money we give her."

"Hmm" was all the sound I could think to make.

Her voice softened a little. "Most of these poor idiots do, you know."

I didn't know.

We'd been there about four weeks when Anna came. She came under cover of darkness, like a thief in the night. She and her four children. She looked behind her all the time and kept her children close. I thought she was planning, every minute, what she would do if HE jumped out at her now. Or now. Or now. I knew how that was. I understood.

"Hi," I greeted her in the hall after a few days there. Her eyes shot up, but noted only that I wasn't HIM before settling back over her children. "My name is Stephanie. I'm two doors over in 1433, if you need anything." I tried to connect. It was impossible. Her mind was just too busy right now. She reached her door, looked over first one shoulder, then the other, and turned the key in the lock.

It was two days after that when I stepped out of my room and saw the men coming out of hers. Men weren't supposed to be on this floor. I slipped back into my room and closed the door.

Gloria was all excited when I got to her office.

"You know that weird woman a couple doors down from you?"

"You mean Anna?"

"Yeah. Anna." She sounded surprised. "You ever talk to her or anything?"

"No," I answered. "Not really."

"Well, get this," she began. Anna, she told me, had come seeking refuge after a fight with her husband of seventeen years. This particular fight had ended when Anna used a baseball bat to send him to the hospital. The police had brought her here when they knew her husband was going to be all right. She'd been terrified. Kept insisting that he was going to kill her. Carolyn, another counselor, believed that Anna had intended to kill him. Anna had mumbled something about his saying if she ever raised a hand to him, she should make damn sure he died, 'cause if he ever got up . . . I don't know if the threatened consequences had been left up to Gloria's imagination or if she was just leaving them up to mine.

"Anyway," Gloria continued, almost breathless. "It seems last night somebody walked right into Lincoln Hospital in the Bronx and stabbed the son of a bitch fourteen times!" She was smiling. My mouth fell open. "So, when the detectives come this morning, I show 'em to her room, open the door with a passkey, and BOOM! No Anna. She's gone — lock, stock, and barrel. Not a trace of her or the kids."

I felt suddenly sick.

"Don't you get it?" She nudged my shoulder. "That's what he gets. It's what he asked for and it's what he gets!"

I didn't get it.

"Oh come on!" She seemed irritated. "You can't keep bleeding for other people. That's how you got into this situation." She touched my shoulder. "Anna's a big girl. She knew what she was doing. So did he."

It was at that moment I became certain the woman at the E.A.U. had been wrong. This place was no place for people like me.

It was another shelter — not the kind for people like me — that found a way to send us back to Indiana. I jumped at the chance.

Contrary to how I'd imagined it a thousand times before, crossing the border into Indiana was not like touching base in a game of hide-and-seek.

It did not make us automatically safe, and it did not end the game.

The kids hated it; they said it was green everywhere. And I resented the poverty in which we lived. It seemed more pronounced here. Even more than the poverty, though, I resented the assumptions people made concerning it.

I had a lot to learn.

I had help.

17

Charity Begins

I PEEPED OUT the window on a cold December morning about a week before Christmas to see a middle-aged man with a soft face and a knee-length black coat waiting expectantly outside my door. He didn't look like welfare — no manila folder or clipboard. He had a grocery bag in his arms. Great. Another 'helper.' I wished these people would just leave us alone. I shushed the kids and watched for a minute as another man came up the stairs to join him. He held a rather heavy-looking box. "No answer?" he asked. The first man shook his head. "You suppose we should leave it on the porch?"

"What's the matter?" someone yelled from down in the street. I saw a woman, gray haired and rosy cheeked, lifting yet another grocery bag from the open trunk of an expensive car just asking for trouble in this neighborhood.

"Nobody home," the second man shouted back.

The disappointment showed in her face and touched me. Something about her said she really wanted to do this. It was against my first instincts, but I opened the door.

Their excitement was catching. They were from some church somewhere, they told me as they bustled back and forth bringing bags, boxes, and baskets. "We didn't get toys for the kids, Ma'am. We were interested in the basics for your family." I wondered if it was the cold that made his teeth chatter.

"Oh," I repeated again and again. "Oh, yes." I didn't know what else to say.

I touched each of them before they left. They looked somehow as if they would like that. "Thank you," I said. Tears filled the woman's eyes and she looked very proud of herself. "Thanks so much to all of you." I tried to look grateful.

"Merry Christmas, Ma'am, God bless your family."

"Oh, yes," I said, turning to the other man. "Thank you too. Tell them all we said thank you. And Merry Christmas." He didn't say anything, but looked at me with watery eyes and nodded.

"He can't wait to get back to his church," I thought. I imagined his telling the others of the stunned look on my face, of little Donny's delight in the beautiful ham, and of our heartfelt gratitude. It would make Christmas a little brighter for all of them, a little Christmasier.

When they had gone, I leaned against the door and stared at all the food in the hallway. Jorgie and Juan giggled and squealed as they jumped back and forth over cases of canned goods. Donny had hold of that tremendous ham and was dragging it out of the red-and-green-ribboned basket. When Vanessa found a tin of cookies, however, they easily abandoned their celebration and followed her into the kitchen

"What're we gonna do with it?" Marie asked after a few minutes.

"Well," I answered. "I don't know. I suppose that whatever doesn't need to be cooked or refrigerated, we're gonna use." I began sorting through the goods, picking out applesauce, bread, more cookies, pretzels, and some of the canned goods: pineapple chunks, corn, pork and beans.

"What about the rest of it?" she wondered.

"I don't know, Marie. We'll just have to see."

"Why'd they bring it here?" I understood her irritation. I thought of a dozen horrible remarks to make about insensitivity, but said only, "They don't know about us, Marie. They were trying to help."

To myself, I couldn't help noting that had any one of them walked just four steps farther, into the kitchen, they would have seen that we had neither stove nor refrigerator.

"We can use all of this stuff I'm setting over here, though," I pointed out. "Why don't you go see if Edna's got a can opener we can borrow."

"You know she's gonna have a can opener." Valerie laughed from the other room, referring to the rumor that Edna ate the cat food she pulled home twice a month from the store in a grocery cart.

An hour later, the girls were in the living room arguing about whether or not Edna did in fact eat cat food. "O.K. You were just over there getting a can opener, right?" Valerie challenged. "Did you see any kind of people food?"

Marie thought about it for a minute. "No," she replied. "But that doesn't mean she eats cat food. We didn't have any food either this morning." I knew what I would do with the excess food.

Edna was elated. She clucked and fussed over the ribboned bundle as though it had been a baby I'd placed in her arms. I was suddenly kind of glad the church had brought us that worthless ham. "Come in." She tugged at my sleeve. "Get out of the cold."

I waited in the dining room while she put it away. "This'll really make it Christmas." I looked around the place, unable to make out her non-stop chatter from the kitchen. A washtub of water sat on newspapers by the table. I stared into it at the plastic daisies, lillies, poinsettias and roses floating on a sea of green leaves. "Oh, I was just washing my artificial flowers." She re-entered the room, smiling almost shyly. "I thought maybe I'd decorate a little." I noticed then that there wasn't a sign of Christmas here. No tree, no gifts, not a ribbon or wrap anywhere. Even *we* had 'art class' chains of red and green construction paper hanging about.

"Do you have to go?" she asked sadly, when I said goodbye.

"Well, I left the kids by themselves."

"Oh yes — those beautiful children," she said, cheering up some. "I watch them from my kitchen window, you know, playing in the back yard."

I smiled.

"Beautiful children," she repeated wistfully as I started for the door. "Just beautiful. That littlest girl reminds me of my Becka when she was little."

"Your daughter?" I asked.

"My youngest," she replied, motioning at the wall above the buffet, at the pictures that hung there. I looked for a while at the two sons and a daughter who were, long since, grown and gone, who'd "never liked artificial flowers," and who never called anymore, never visited, and wrote only a few lines on a card a couple times a year. She pointed to one lying on the buffet. "That's all I've heard of Becka all year." I wasn't sure how to look at her. I said nothing. "Excuse me while I get some tissue," she sniffed finally. "I have to blow my nose."

Under my breath, I cursed all the damned insensitive people in the world. I picked up the card and saw on the front the most recent picture of Becka. I wondered, as I looked at her smiling face, what she would think if she knew that strangers were providing what her mother needed.

Love you Mom. Talk to you soon. Happy Hanukkah. Becka.

"Edna wasn't exaggerating about the notes being short," I thought to myself. "This was hardly . . ." I stopped short and looked at the card again. *Happy Hanukkah?!* I felt my face turn red. I'd just given this woman a ham for Christmas, and worse, I'd felt really good about it. Thought I was doing something wonderful.

For the first time, I noticed a delicious smell coming from the kitchen; definitely not cat food. What had I been thinking? I'd been thinking exactly what I wanted to think — whatever made me feel good. I thought, now, of the church people who'd brought me the ham that morning. I was no better than they. They couldn't see what I really needed. Maybe they couldn't have done anything about it if they had. Here I was, just like them, getting rid of my surplus and feeling good about myself in the process.

Unlike them, however, I had stumbled upon a chance to see what it was this dear old woman really needed, and, poor or not, I just happened to have some.

At the sound of her footsteps, I hurriedly replaced the card on the buffet.

"I'm glad I didn't run you off with my sniveling." She smiled, coming out of the kitchen. "I'm sorry about that."

"Oh, no. Don't be." I tried to look solemn. "I stayed because I have to say something. I'm afraid I didn't make myself clear when I came in."

She looked puzzled.

"What I mean is . . . I came here with the intention of asking you . . . That is . . . Edna, I came here to make a deal. You see, I don't have a stove at home, and I thought that maybe if you didn't have any other plans, and if I provided the food, maybe you would be willing to cook it here and we could all have Christmas dinner together."

She stared at me in disbelief.

"I know it's a lot to ask," I went on, "and I'll understand . . ."

Edna put her hand up to quiet me, and excused herself to go for more tissue.

I'd left New York and escaped a monster.

Eventually, of course, I had to face the other monsters — those who'd been waiting for me and those I'd brought back with me.

It started with my brother's persistant resentment of our father. I saw no reason for it. The problems our father had had with his wives were between him and his wives. He'd been good to us. He was, by no means, a monster.

He was no monster who held me when I missed my mother, whose tears wet my scalp as he rocked me and kissed my forehead, stroking my cheek and whispering that everything would be all right. He was no monster who hurt his tooth biting down, in frustration, on the hairpins he held awkwardly in his mouth as he clumsily twisted the locks of my wet hair into curls around his thick stubby fingers; whose eyes filled and voice cracked as he agreed to do it, always, "just like Mommie used to do it." He was no monster whose face melted in confused heartache when I cried because Danny Hoss didn't like me or who, much later, yelped in shocked panic when I appeared on his doorstep wearing the two black eyes my new husband had given me. He was no monster who pulled at his hair in helpless agony when I threatened never to speak to him again if he dared do anything about it.

18

Our Two Fathers

IT'S HARD TO say how it was that I loved my father as easily and completely as I did. Or why I was so blind to the reasons that other people didn't.

It seemed to me that they should all be able to overlook the things that had happened so long ago. Forgive and forget, I said. I mean, I certainly wouldn't want to be held in disdain for *my* childhood misdeeds.

And while my father was by no means a child at the time, we were all a lot younger then.

I'd left New York to escape a monster.

Eventually, of course, I had to face the other monsters — those who'd been here waiting for me, and those I'd brought back with me.

I began with my brother.

We were alone in Grandma's living room, Thanksgiving dinner behind us, and the kids out in the backyard providing much-needed exercise for Grandma's dog.

I alternated between staring at the TV and watching my brother stare at it. I wondered for the zillionth time why Debbie hadn't showed up. It was bordering on the rude for her to leave me stranded here alone with Don. She knew how he felt about me, how we offended each other. Par for the course, I supposed. I knew that the rudeness, the insults and offenses, that somehow wove our family together, were far too complicated ever to have been intentional.

He must've felt my stare; he turned to me. "What?" he asked dryly.

"Nothing," I replied. "I was just noticing how much you look like Daddy."

He grimaced, disgusted, and looked back at the TV.

Why did he always do stuff like that, I wondered. Why did he have to be such a jerk, always so hard against Daddy? Would he never just forgive and forget?

I stared intentionally now — hard. He remained lost in the TV and refused to notice me. I thought how different we were, how purposely alone he always seemed to keep himself, how removed, resentful, and how relentless in his disdain for our father. And then, as I sat there trying with all my might to stare a hole in the side of his face, something happened. My memory took over and I noticed something I was sure hadn't been there earlier. I recognized, suddenly, someone I hadn't seen in a long time. Someone I'd once cared for very much; I saw my brother in that face. Not the angry man who stared at the TV set, but my brother. The little boy with whom I'd shared a set of parents, a household and a childhood. I recognized, for just an instant, the face of a child. And for just that instant I glimpsed an expression I'd seen so many years before, and which I'd somehow forgotten.

It was Christmas morning. I was ten years old. Debbie and I woke up first and hit the stairs running, neck and neck, not officially racing, but each one struggling to pull ahead of the other by just an inch, and each one keeping a firm hand on the other one's shoulder, ready to shove her sideways should she begin to take the lead. As we rounded the landing, the sight of the colored Christmas tree lights reflected on the wall below excited me no end, and I shoved Debbie. She bumped the banister and lost momentum, but not enough. I was three steps from the bottom when she grabbed my hair. I went backward and she came forward, and we spilled down the last of the stairs together. She started toward the tree even before she was in an upright position. I pulled her back by the hem of her nightgown. Finally we armed and legged, and scooted and rolled our way into the living room, more or less together.

It was paradise. There were Barbies and accessories everywhere. And a 'Hi, Heidi' doll who was supposed to wave 'Hi' if you pressed her stomach, but whose jerky gesture more closely resembled the greeting of the Nazi party. There was a Skipper doll and a radio and more — too much stuff to see all at once.

It wasn't until I noticed the life-size, authentic-looking military gun sitting on a tripod right in the way of my Barbie Dream House, that I realized that Donny wasn't down here yet.

I looked around the room again. This time with an eye for what had to be his, the boy things. There were gobs of them. G.I. Joes, trucks, cowboys, guns, and all sorts of boy junk littering the beautiful doll clothes and buggies and stuffed-animal radios. And he hadn't seen any of it yet. I looked at Debbie. She hadn't thought of it; she was busy. I resisted the impulse to go over and snatch away whatever it was that interested her so, and instead, got quietly to my feet and crept, stealthily, from the room.

Halfway to the landing I glanced behind me. Ha! Debbie hadn't even noticed I was gone. I was thrilled. I was going to get to tell him. Besides getting presents yourself, telling somebody else about theirs was the best part of Christmas.

He lay on his side facing the wall, his knees slightly bent and his back to me. I scrunched up my shoulders to keep from laughing out loud and took long, tip-toed steps over to his bed.

"Don-ny," I whispered musically, trying to sound mysterious. I picked a string of tinsel from the bottom of my sock and let it dangle down onto his cheek. "Oh Don-ny," I giggled.

"What," he answered, without moving, and in a voice so crisp, dry, and perfectly straight that I knew he had not been asleep. I was a little annoyed. I twisted myself over him to see his face.

"What're you doin'?" I asked.

He didn't answer, but continued to stare straight ahead. His eyes looked strange. I couldn't tell if they were full, like maybe he saw something I couldn't see, or if they were empty, and he was seeing nothing at all. I looked at the wall where he stared, and back at him again, confused. He seemed somehow smarter than I at that moment.

"Santa Claus came," I said, straightening myself up and bumping the side of his mattress with my knees. He didn't move. I bent over him again. "You've been real good this year."

He had. Even I had noticed he'd stopped being a crybaby.

He didn't respond. I wondered if maybe he was still afraid. I knew about the fear. I had been afraid too, at first. Afraid of life without Mommie, wondering what Daddy might do to me. But that was over now. Everything had turned out fine. No more fights and screaming all the time.

Daddy wasn't mad anymore—except, sometimes, at Donny.

I tried not to think about that, though. I always tried not to notice whenever Daddy called him "Sissy" or "Punk." Or when he threatened or kicked him. I didn't want to notice. I guess I was just glad it wasn't me.

I looked, that Christmas morning, at that face, and saw the ultimate in disappointment. Donny had waited all these months for something that, he now knew, wasn't coming. It was Christmas. She wasn't here. It was final.

He looked so sweet and so sad. I was briefly amazed that this chubby little face could piss Daddy off so bad.

"I want to stop being here," he said, quietly and evenly. I wasn't sure he meant me to hear.

"What!?" I asked. "That's crazy! Where else would you be?" I wore an exaggerated look of confusion, but deep down inside me, somewhere near the pit of my stomach, some part of me fluttered and I knew what he meant. I ignored it.

"I don't want it to be Christmas," he whispered.

"Come on, Donny." I stood up straight and bumped the mattress again. "At least come and see what Santa Claus brought."

"I already did," he said slowly, closing his eyes in some new blend of anger and agony.

He refused to move or talk anymore, no matter what I did, and I finally gave up and went downstairs.

A few minutes later, I sat on the floor furiously squeezing Heidi's body into Skipper's clothes.

"What's the matter with Donny?" Debbie asked, forcing me to think of that face upstairs. That horrible, suffering, un-Christmas face. It connected somehow to my own feelings and made me sad and uncomfortable. It threatened me and I didn't like it. So I handled it the only way I knew — I ignored it.

"I don't know." I shrugged. "I guess he didn't get what he wanted for Christmas."

I looked now at the face of the man lost in the TV set, and felt tremendous guilt. How could I have just shoved those things aside for so long? My father had been good to me and I couldn't hate him, but my God, surely I had owed it to Donny not to have forgotten; at the very least to have acknowledged his pain. But I hadn't. He had been alone in it all. And he had done well, turned out fine, despite all of it. He hadn't gone whacko or anything. Here he sat, watching TV, an honest, hard working man, who maybe drank too much, but who, for the most part, never bothered anybody.

I was ashamed. Who was I to tell this man whom to forgive, and what to get over? Hell, he had a right, perhaps even an obligation, to be just as mad as he wanted to be.

The face looked back at me, and I wondered if my little brother was still in there somewhere. I thought that he must be. He couldn't really have stopped being there, could he?

I had an almost irresistible urge to touch this face now, to say, "I love you, Donny." I wanted to tell him that I was sorry Mommie had left him, that Daddy had hurt him, and most of all, that I had forgotten. I wanted to say, "I remember now, Donny, and I love you."

I didn't, though. I didn't say anything. I knew the time for all that had passed.

I blamed his memory of this incident on his self-involvement and lack of understanding. It hadn't happened that way, I told myself. I refused to

remember a father who kicked and shoved my brother around outside the house, and who slapped and dragged my sister around inside.

I like to think, now, that it was for noble reasons I didn't remember. I didn't want to drag it up anymore. I just wanted to love my father. But no. That's not the truth. The truth is that my father was different. Oh, he was that same man, but he was not that same father. No, my father was no monster — to me.

My brother's father, unfortunately, was every bit a monster.

I really hate that.

And what's worse is that, even right now, faced with the facts, with undeniable memories staring me in the eye, I cannot do else but love my father. Even realizing what a mean and hurtful soul he once was, a sadistic man who severely damaged my siblings; even knowing that my mother would likely be alive today if not for her involvement with him, I love my father. And I miss him more than words can say.

It's a sickness, I suppose, but one I've learned to live with.

19

Ruthie

SHE HAD OBVIOUSLY been placed on the bed; the position was not one she would have assumed herself. Most of the tubes were gone, only the morphine and oxygen remained. Thank God she'd had the foresight to refuse tube feeding. She would be allowed to starve to death. It wouldn't be long now. The five-month ordeal was coming to a close. Three days, they said. Five months ago they had said she would be dead within a month. They couldn't understand why she hung on as she did.

Ruthie was not our real mother. She had been given to us, much the way a present is given, when I was twelve years old.

"You guys come out here," my dad had called from the living room one July night. 'I've got a surprise for you." It was Ruthie. Some of us liked her; some of us didn't. We all got used to her. She had staying power. If she knew that my father had married her only as a babysitter/housekeeper to help him maintain legal custody of his children, she didn't seem to mind. Our lives changed with Ruthie. We ate better, our clothes were clean, our house gradually lost that unidentifiable smell.

For a while, my dad's life went on pretty much as usual; he would stop in every few days, usually in the middle of the night, bombed, carrying a bucket of chicken and ready to dance, only now it was Ruthie, not us, who waltzed groggily around the living room, to a rhythm planted in his head by the jukebox in the last bar. It never annoyed her. The sound of his key in the lock, regardless of time, would trigger the zipper of her make-up bag, and she would head for the bathroom. I don't think he ever saw her without frosty pink lipstick complementing her straight, white teeth. I hid the corny pleasure I felt watching them dance. He was strong and handsome. She was beautiful. Loretta Lynn hair puffed off her forehead to hang, long and black, down her back. I didn't even mind that he never danced with me anymore.

My father began to drink less and less. He was around the house more. His relationship with Ruthie took on strange characteristics. He began to tell her jokes. He told her things that happened at work. They discussed his problems. A respect of some sort blossomed.

His need for Ruthie continued to increase, long after his need for a babysitter/housekeeper had expired. Despite his "citiness," my father and his wife grew to be one person the way only old-fashioned, down-home couples can.

When the invader first struck, she tried to ignore it in the hope it would go away. She didn't want him to know. They had no health insurance. He would worry.

It didn't go away. She stood up from her bed one morning and her hip fell apart. "C-C-Cancer." She stumbled over the 'C' word on the telephone in her hospital room.

"Promise me," she whispered later. "Please don't let this hurt your father." I didn't want to promise anything. I didn't want to talk about it. "Promise me, Stephie," she insisted. "Promise that you'll . . . you know . . . do something for me. Don't let it get bad . . . please." She was talking about morphine — an accidental overdose.

"I promise." I had believed at the time that I could do it, but, five months later, like my father, I was repeating silly "goodbyes" to someone too involved in dying to know or care what I said.

They sold everything they had, and cashed in their life insurance policies to cover medical costs. She just kept dying.

My father knelt at her bedside again. "I'm sorry, Baby." It didn't sound like his voice. "I just can't," he whispered. "Please understand. Forgive me." His hand, careful not to break anything, was on hers as he pleaded. I'd seen my father cry before, but this was different; he didn't cry now. He was beyond that. He'd made and broken the same promise I had.

I didn't have the courage to do what she'd asked. I couldn't put a stop to it. It was against the law. Wrong. Instead, I watched the metamorphosis. I watched my father watch. I remembered her rushing to put on lipstick.

His face never quite adjusted. He never stopped displaying astonishment, shocked despair, at her appearance. I shared his guilt. The Loretta Lynn hair was all but gone; a few strands straggled here and there. The lips were gone too, stretched tight over teeth huge now by comparison. Her tongue was little more than a raisin lying in the dry, gaping hole, smelling of moldy fruit that had once been her mouth.

I hoped she did not know what she was now — an undead corpse in the process of decomposition, smiling a hideous death grin, while empty bones splintered and cracked.

I wondered, every minute of the seven final days it took her to die, what it feels like to starve to death.

She weighed seventy-eight pounds when she died; my father weighed ninety-four. Forty days after her death, haunted by her agony, he died, overdosed on morphine. He said he'd always thought he would go first, get a chance to make it up to her. Said he couldn't live with his inadequacy as a husband; that he should've been able to do something for her — end her misery. It wasn't right, he said. He felt he'd let her down.

I know.

That's when the question of responsibility for the monsters came back to me. I was certain my father hadn't wanted to be a monster. He wasn't, to me, but there was no denying the fact he had been every bit a monster to my little brother.

The question was odd. If he was so good to me, was he a monster indeed? How about what he was to my mother? Did I have a right to forget it and love him as I did? Or was I somehow obliged to remember the bad things, even forgetting the good, as some form of punishment to him?

These are all questions that go far beyond my ability to answer with any degree of confidence. Something happened a little later, however, that helped me to, if not answer them, at least see them in a new light.

20

The Good Demon

I HEARD SOMETHING rustle in the kitchen. The clock read two fifteen.

"Luis, is that you?"

"Yeah," he replied.

I was getting into my robe when he whispered through the door, "Are you up, Mom?"

We sat in the living room, he on the floor, I on the couch.

"Another dream?" I asked. He nodded. "Can you talk about it?" He shrugged his shoulders.

Maybe he has nightmares every night, since he got out of the state school for boys. If so, he doesn't show it. Only once or twice a month does he wake up, sweating, in the middle of the night.

I don't know how often or how horribly a person ought to remember these kinds of things, but I know very well that he shouldn't forget.

I get up with him when he is tormented by his dreams. I listen when he can talk. I long to comfort him, tell him it isn't real, only a dream, but I can't.

The dreams aren't about the correctional facility. Neither are they about going back, as he first claimed. They are about things that happened before he went away, before he got caught. He dreams, now, of things he did, back then, when he was still "hangin' with the guys."

My son has replaced his father as the demon of his own nightmares. He is plagued by memories. Things I can't imagine.

Perhaps people who've never been the monster, good people, don't realize all that's involved. How tough it must be to deny the sound of one's own humanity ringing in the cries of another. The monster's mind must be ever vigilant, moving constantly, lest it stop for a second and recognize itself in the terrified babblings of the victim. For if that happens, the dreams come.

"He had a confused *Why me?* look on his face," Luis whispers, remembering something I never knew. "He just sat there in the middle of the street, his nose pouring blood, his groceries scattered from one curb to the other, and looked at us." I look at my son, not knowing what to say, torn between a desire to comfort him and a sense of justice in his torment. I am glad he doesn't tell me what happened next, but shakes his head, instead, into his hands. "We humiliated him so bad. The poor guy was just tryin' to get home with his groceries." His voice trails off wistfully, pensive.

"Probably to his family," I whisper. He winces and I hate myself. "To his kids," I add with some sick pleasure. He squinches his eyes and covers his ears. I wonder, briefly, what kind of mother I must be, to do such a thing.

I know that my son, my baby, is in absolute torment. I know it and my heart aches for him. I want to make it better. I believe that I can; there are things that could be said. But I don't say them. I don't say them because I am a human being. Even before I am a mother, I am a human being, and the image he draws for me—that poor man sitting helpless in the middle of the street—he draws too well. I can see the man's face, feel his fear. He has come alive and he will not let me comfort my son. He has stepped out of my child's dreams, out of his past to haunt me too.

In daylight, I wonder if perhaps the man hasn't long since forgotten the incident; he wasn't injured. Or perhaps he thinks of it only on occasion, and then without any guilt or self-loathing; with a clear villain onto which to target his hatred. With all my heart, I hope this is the case.

My son, on the other hand, will never forget. And it will never be all right.

I marvel that sometimes — just sometimes — the world secretly works exactly as it should.

[ ]

Once a monster, always a monster?

Should parents/spouses/children ever just forgive and forget?

How are monsters made?

I don't know, I don't know, and I don't know.

Monsters, it turns out, are very complicated things. Seems any one of us might be a monster or a victim, or the creator of a monster or a victim, depending on what day you talk to us.

I'm glad, on some level, that my son is tormented. It's the sort of thing that'll take the monster out of him.

I believe that's what happened to my father. Whatever he was in his life, in the end he was no monster. My siblings and I are agreed on that.

As for Lou, I don't know if he remained a monster after I left him; he certainly wasn't my monster anymore. I can't even guess what he might be doing now. Nothing would surprise me.

Out Of The Woods

HERE'S ANOTHER STORY by my friend Gary, whose account of the dog on the railroad track suggested what it feels like to be a battered woman. This story mirrors how it feels to be me — now. I listened to Gary tell this childhood experience to a few people at a party:

When he was still a very little boy, Gary went to an event at a local park with his much older sister and her fiancé. The sister and fiancé were young, in love, and completely caught up in each other, leaving Gary pretty much on his own. He was drawn to a huge collapsible table set up near a wooded area. Beside the table was a shiny red bike with a tag on the handlebars. On the table was an assortment of toys and games, all brand new, still in the packages. His eyes rolled over them to the end—to the electric-train set. It was beautiful, exactly what he'd always wanted. In awe, he reached toward it.

"Don't touch the prizes," someone shouted at him.

"Prizes?" he thought to himself hopefully. He wondered how he might get a shot at that train set.

Just then someone blew a whistle and more kids than he'd ever seen at one time began lining up side by side behind a white line chalked on the grass over in front of the picnic tables. He ran for it, and squeezed into the line just as a man standing off to one side raised a pistol in the air. The starting shot rang out and Gary was off with the bang.

It was at the entrance to the woods when he felt himself pull away from the others. He was far too nervous to look, however, until he was well into the woods. Then he stole only a quick glance over each shoulder and realized to his delight there wasn't a soul in sight. He ran even faster, visions of the train set spinning in his head. He hurdled stumps and dodged trees left and right, ignoring the branches and vines that scratched at his arms and legs and slapped at his face. A chubby boy, he'd never been particularly fast, but today he felt just like the wind. No one could catch him as he emerged from the woods at top speed, slowed, and finally came to a stop just short of the street. He didn't see a finish line, but felt sure he wasn't expected to cross the street. He turned and looked back at the trees — still no one. He raised his hands in victory, throwing that silly basket they'd given him to the ground. It would take more than that little basket to carry the prize he had his eye on. He leaned now, resting his hands on his knees, and struggled for breath. His legs ached, his eyes burned, and his lungs were about to burst, but it didn't matter; he had won. He was a winner. He watched the edge of the woods, as he pulled in air, for whoever would come in second. He would greet and congratulate the lucky guy, gloating only a little and not at all noticeably. He wondered, as he watched and breathed, if he would get to pick his prize or if it would be assigned to him.

Seconds became minutes and still no one came out of those woods. When it became evident that no one would come — no one could be that slow — he started back the way he had come, wondering what on earth could have happened to everyone.

He was about halfway through the patch of trees when he heard the voices of children.

"Look under that clump there!" was followed shortly by excited giggles and a shout of "Oh! I found another one. I got three!"

Peering curiously in the direction of the voices, he saw a little girl, smaller than he by a full head, placing a blue egg in her basket. Other kids — all of them — were wandering around, lifting rocks and clumps of leaves, searching.

By the time Gary figured out what was going on, and what to do about it, all the Easter eggs, and his hopes for any prize at all, were gone. He came out of the woods exactly where he had gone in, and stood quietly by his sister as the prizes were handed out.

She was puzzled when she noticed him.

"Oh, I didn't play," he explained, faking an uninterested yawn. "They only had dumb prizes — nothing I'd want."

As Gary told this story, several people, and in fact, Gary himself, laughed in amusement. I couldn't. I'd heard, in that simple little story, my life.

I'd seen myself in that little boy, struggling for all I was worth toward the prizes, hurrying to get a husband, a baby, a family; rushing, rushing, rushing madly, without any idea of how to get the prizes. Not even knowing that I didn't know.

I couldn't laugh at the story. I cried. I cried and I couldn't stop. "Hey," Gary smiled, a little amused, and perhaps a little embarrassed by my tears. "C'mon. It's not such a sad story. I got over it."

I pressed a tissue to my eyes and tried to stop, but the story had made me think. I thought about how my own story could have ended, and I shuddered.

I tried to smile. He was right, I knew. He was right. Perhaps that's why I couldn't stop crying; perhaps such great relief is uncontrollable. And that's what I'd found in that simple story: a tremendous relief. I realized, suddenly, how very damned lucky I am to have turned around when I did, to have gotten back into the hunt, basket in hand, before all the eggs were gone.

I saw, in that little boy, the truth about my own story. That despite the bad beginning, the scary middle, and all the might-have-beens, despite the odds and the dreadful predictions, despite everything pointing to the contrary, it's not such a sad story after all.